World War One: A Layman's Guide

by

Scott Addington

©Scott Addington 2012

Ink And Incredibility: Not Another History Of The First World War!

There is one person to blame for yet another history on the First World War, his name is Duncan and he is a tattooist from Area51 tattoo studio in Basingstoke. He is responsible for the tattoo I have on the inside of my lower right arm. The ink in question depicts WW1 soldiers going over the top, it is a very famous image taken from a still of a movie made at the time. Nothing unusual in this I guess, given my background and interest in this particular phase of world history.

What is slightly more unusual is the fact that, when I wear short sleeves, I get stopped several times a day by complete strangers who want to talk about my tattoo. The conversation typically goes something like this:

(Stranger) "Hey! I love your tattoo; I have not seen anything like that before"

(Me) "Thank you, yes I guess it is pretty unique, I haven't seen anyone with a similar design"

(Stranger) "What is it exactly?"

(Me) "It is depicting British soldiers going over the top during WW1"

(Stranger) "That is amazing. I think my <insert deceased family member> fought in the First World War. I don't really know much about what he did though. It's a shame; I should really find out a bit more."

(Me) "So why don't you then? There are hundreds of books on WW1, pick a couple up and get reading!"

(Stranger) "Yeah, I should, but all the books I have seen look too <insert any one of the following: complicated/boring/dull/technical/long/heavy/difficult to understand> and I just don't have the time to read anything these days, life is so busy!"

So, it seems that despite the plethora of literature that has already been written on the First World War, there is still a large number of people (in the south of England at least) that would like to know more but for one reason or another think that the majority of existing literature is not written for them.

This got me thinking.

I am not a historian, and for many that could be a big problem, because I do not have the intimate knowledge of the subject that an academic heavyweight would. But wait. Perhaps that isn't such a bad thing after all. Perhaps something that was written, not by an academic, but by an ordinary 'Layman' would work here; using very short, sharp chapters that could take people who have little or no prior knowledge of the First World War through the main areas of the conflict to give them at least a passing knowledge of the more salient points. It would have to be written in a more conversational style and must be written in a way that can succinctly describe the main points of a serious piece of military history, not in 900 pages, but in 900 words. Something that could be dipped in an out when time permits, but didn't mean you had to re-read the last five pages to try and remember where you had originally got up to.

Here is that 'something'. It doesn't pretend to be academic in nature, (think of it more like a conversation over a pint), it doesn't pretend to be the last word on the subject, it doesn't pretend to cover everything in exhaustive detail, it is unashamedly bias towards the Western Front and it hasn't uncovered anything new or ground breaking. Indeed, people who hold a decent knowledge of the subject should perhaps walk away and read something else as you are not the intended audience. It does however try to give a new spin on current content and thoughts around the First World War and deliver it in a sharp, easy-to-dip-in-and-out way in an effort to make what can be a very daunting subject easier to digest and understand, especially for people who are reading about the subject for the first time.

Welcome then, to *The First World War: A Layman's Guide*.

Contents:

The German Master Strategy: The Schlieffen Plan.

In 1892, two of Germany's largest military rivals, France and Russia, joined hands and signed an alliance that left Germany feeling a little... well, threatened. If anything kicked off with either country, Germany would be facing a war on two fronts very quickly, which, let's be honest, was not an appealing prospect.

So, the German military brains got thinking on how best to deal with any future issues that could arise due to this new alliance and in 1899 Kaiser Wilhelm II approved the first draft of their master plan. Conjured up by Count Alfred von Schlieffen, it was basically a pre-emptive strike on France if and when things turned a bit naughty with Russia. The basic thinking was this: If any kind of war emerged it would take both France and Germany about fifteen days to be ready to fight a decisive battle, however it would take the Russians about six weeks to be ready for a fight, so in theory that gave Germany six weeks to kill off the French, get back to Germany and prepare their eastern front for the Russian attacks.

Piece of Cake.

Of course, with all the French fortresses dotted around the Franco-German border, such as those at Verdun, it would be unlikely such a quick victory would be attained in a head on assault. Switzerland wasn't really a viable route into France either due to its mountainous and difficult terrain, but Belgium, with its wide flat countryside, offered a very real possibility for the likely invasion route. Belgium was neutral, so going through her would technically be illegal, but which war was ever 100% above board? And so it was decided. A massive invasion of Belgium would brush their army aside as the German forces marched south into France and around the back of Paris, sweeping through the capital and back towards the border, encircling the French Army en route. The attack would be swift and calculating. So fast, in-fact, that Great Britain, the historical protector of Belgian neutrality, would have barely finished a cup of tea before the Germans were partying in Paris. Or at least, that was the plan.

Between 1899 and 1906 this master plan crystallised into a very precise order of battle. Thirty-four divisions, backed up by heavy artillery, would invade Belgium and move down into France towards Lille. Meanwhile a smaller force would hold onto the Franco-German border in case the French decided that the best form of defence was attack. These frontier armies would then slowly retreat into Germany, pulling the French with them, leaving a big hole behind, which the invading forces would fill, surround the attacking French forces and destroy them. Once the French were out of the way the focus could then switch to the east.

In 1906, von Schlieffen was replaced as Chief-of-Staff by Field Marshall Helmuth von Moltke. When it was clear that war was imminent in the summer of 1914, von Moltke set the plan in motion. However, he made one small, but ultimately costly, change to the original plans; he was very nervous about the build-up of French forces on their border and took significant troops and resources away from the northern wing of his forces and placed them opposite the French.

In the end, when the 'go' button was ultimately pressed, this would prove very costly.

The Spark That Lit a Thousand Fires: The Assassination of Archduke Franz Ferdinand.

28th June 1914. Archduke Franz Ferdinand had an appointment in Bosnia to oversee some army manoeuvres. He didn't expect to be welcomed with open arms on this trip, the Archduke was the heir to the throne of the ruling Austro-Hungarian Empire, and a large percentage of the Bosnian population were unhappy at Austrian dominance, instead favouring a union with Serbia. Despite being royally despised, the Archduke was looking forward to the trip and his party arrived by train at around 10am.

At 10.10am when the six car possession passed the central police station, Nedjelko Cabrinovic, a member of a local terrorist group called 'Black Hand' hurled a hand grenade at the Archduke's car. The driver accelerated when he saw the object flying towards him and the grenade exploded under the wheel of the next car. Two of the occupants, Eric von Merizzi and Count Boos-Waldeck were seriously wounded. About a dozen spectators were also hit by bomb splinters.

The Archduke's driver, Franz Urban, drove on extremely fast and other members of the Black Hand group on the route were unable to fire their guns or hurl their bombs at the Archduke's car. After attending the official reception at the City Hall Ferdinand asked about the wounded members of his party, when told they were badly injured and in hospital he insisted on being taken to see them.

General Oskar Potiorek decided that it would be safer if the royal car should avoid the city centre on its way to the Sarajevo

Hospital. However, Potiorek forgot to tell the driver, Franz Urban, about this decision. On the way to the hospital Urban took a right turn into Franz Joseph Street. One of the conspirators, Gavrilo Princip, was standing on the corner at the time. Potiorek immediately realised the driver had taken the wrong route and shouted for him to stop.

Urban stopped and began to back up. In doing so he moved slowly past the waiting Princip. The assassin stepped forward, drew his gun, and at a distance of about five feet fired several times into the car. Ferdinand was hit in the neck and his wife, the Duchess, was hit in the abdomen. Princip's bullet had pierced the Archduke's jugular vein but before losing consciousness, he pleaded "Sophie dear! Sophie dear! Don't die! Stay alive for our children!" Franz Urban drove the royal couple to Konak, the governor's residence, but although both were still alive when they arrived, they died from their wounds soon afterwards.

To put it mildly, this really upset the Austrians, they wanted retribution, and fast. Exactly one month later on the 28th July 1914, Austria declared war on Serbia. Over the next few months a great deal of political pushing and shoving effectively split Europe into two distinct groups of belligerents, each side beating their chest in a show of confidence and military power.

It would only end in tears. And death, lots of death.

Peacocks & Chess Moves: Prelude to War

After the assassination of the Archduke there began a period of political bicep flexing and a flurry of pacts, friendly handshakes and aggressive finger pointing as the major (and some of the not so major) powers of Europe shuffled themselves into two distinct sides ready for what would be an August face-off.

On 6th July, Germany put an arm around its Austro-Hungarian cousins and told them they could count on German support if they decided on revenge against Serbia. Indeed, Germany, (who had become increasingly nervous of Russia over the last number of years) saw this as a good opportunity to put Russia back in her rightful place... But, if Germany had any hopes of defeating Russia in a war they had to act now. Her main ally, Austria-Hungary was threatening to implode and Russia was becoming stronger all the time. It was time to put the wheels in motion.

Germany persistently whispered into the ear of Austria-Hungary, suggesting that the Serbian government were behind the assassination. On the 9th Friedrich von Wiesner, an official from the Austro-Hungarian Foreign Office was sent to check it out. Not surprisingly, four days later on 14th July, Herr von Wiesner reported back confirming the rumours that the Serbia government were indeed behind the assassination. Now the Austro-Hungarians were jumping up and down with rage. It was time for action.

On the 21st July the Chief-of-Staff of the Austro-Hungarian Army, Conrad von Hotzendorff, called for the declaration of war on Serbia claiming that no one in Europe would bat an eyelid. Feeling brave two days later on the 23rd July, the Austro-Hungarian government placed fifteen separate demands on the Serbian government, including one that they arrest the leaders of the Black Hand and send them to Vienna for trial.

The next day, the 24th July, fearing the worst, the Serbs asked Russia for their help if they were to be attacked by Austria-Hungary. They got the nod from the Russians on the 26th July. Meanwhile they had already stuck two fingers up at Austria-Hungary by flatly refusing to co-operate with any of their demands. This didn't really go down well with Emperor Franz Josef and the rest of the Austro-Hungarians, and they duly declared war on Serbia on the 28th July.

On the 31st July Russia mobilised her army in support of Serbia, and in a provocative move, rushed a large number of troops right up to the borders of Austria-Hungary and Germany.

This was an invitation Germany could not ignore and duly declared war on Russia 24 hours later, citing aggressive Russian behaviour and the need to protect their territory from any impending threat. However, the Germans were also very nervous about France. If Germany committed to a war with Russia in the east, Germany's western flank would be vulnerable to French attack. The German plan to overcome this perceived threat was laid out in their Schlieffen Plan. German thinking at this time was that the French army was relatively weak and could be defeated before the much stronger Russians had fully mobilised. If this could be achieved they would then be free to concentrate on Russia without the threat of an attack on their western front. As such Germany declared war on France on 3rd August. They were now committed to something they were originally trying to avoid; a war on two fronts.

Now it was time for Britain to get in on the act. When Germany declared war on France, Belgium understandably felt uneasy. As a neutral territory they looked to Britain to help them preserve their position. Britain, being generally nice chaps, immediately tipped their hat to Belgium and guaranteed to protect their neutrality. In the same breath Britain warned Germany that if they set foot in Belgium they could consider themselves at war with Britain and her Empire.

It was all about to kick off big time. The Germans walked straight into Belgium on the 4th August and true to their word Britain declared war on Germany. Over the next ten days or so, all the major protagonists declared war on each other, making two very distinct, very powerful and very destructive sides; led by Austria-Hungary and Germany on one side, and Russia, France and Great Britain on the other.

After all this political showboating and feather ruffling it would be left to the ordinary man in the street to fight it out in the trenches over the next five years; to live and to die amongst the mud, the guns, the filth, the gas, the rats and the blood.

That Contemptible Little Army: The BEF

After the Second Boer War had ended in 1902, the British Minister for War, Richard Haldane, spearheaded a reform of the British Army. Hindered by a nation obsessed with its Navy and a political system opposed to conscription, the opportunity to grow the army was limited, so Haldane concentrated on modernisation and training, with the aim of building an elite force of 6 infantry divisions and 1 cavalry division, all available for rapid mobilisation as a British Expeditionary Force (BEF) in mainland Europe, backed, if needed, by a reserve of fourteen Territorial divisions of volunteers.

The overseas portion of the British Army – specifically those armies in India, Egypt, South Africa and the Middle East were the big losers in this re-structure. Despite the fact that over half of the total strength of the army was stationed overseas, these forces were often starved of men, equipment and resources in order to bolster the BEF.

At the outbreak of war in August 1914 the BEF was about 120,000 strong and ready to go. They had seen the European heavyweights poke each other in the eye and were ready to get stuck in. Unfortunately, whilst they were expertly trained (especially in the use of the rifle, at which they were probably the best in the world), they were trained for a mobile war and did not have huge numbers of artillery, machine guns, mortars or grenades.

So, with big smiles and a sense of adventure, the BEF boarded trains and headed off to the fight. The sentiment of the time was that it would 'all be over by Christmas' and it will all be a jolly good escapade. However when they landed in France they marched straight towards an enemy that had already forced the army of Belgium to run and hide. Germany was hugely superior in men and equipment with more artillery, more bombs, and more shells than anyone else in Europe at that time. She also knew how to 'dig in' and form strong defensive positions.

Despite the odds, the BEF put up a great fight and frustrated the on-rushing German army. This can be seen clearly in the famous "Order of the Day" given by the Kaiser, Wilhelm II, on the 19th August, 1914:

"It is my Royal and Imperial Command that you concentrate your energies,

for the immediate present upon one single purpose,

and that is that you address all your skill and all the valour of my soldiers,

to exterminate first, the treacherous English,

walk over General French's contemptible little Army."

With typical British humour, the BEF gladly embraced being called contemptible, and from that day on they would be forever known as 'The Old Contemptibles'.

Despite fighting heroically in the face of vastly superior numbers of men and guns, the original BEF was practically wiped out by the end of 1914, although it had managed to halt the German Army and put a very large British spanner in the works of the Schlieffen Plan.

The survivors of 'The Old Contemptibles' were rightly proud of what they had achieved in 1914. In 1925 Captain John Patrick Danny of the Royal Field Artillery founded The Old Contemptibles Association for veterans of the BEF. At its height it had 178 UK branches, fourteen overseas branches and produced its own magazine.

The Big Kick Off: Mons

Just a matter of weeks after declaring war on Germany, 80,000 members of the BEF along with 30,000 horses and 315 guns of assorted size and calibre had landed in France and were unwittingly marching straight towards the enemy, who had already passed through Luxembourg and was now putting Belgium to the sword. The German Schlieffen plan was working beautifully.

On 22nd August, a forward patrol of the 4th Royal Irish Dragoon Guards encountered the enemy for the first time. While conducting a reconnaissance along the road heading out from Maisières, four enemy cavalrymen of the 2nd Kuirassiers emerged from the direction of Casteau. They were spotted by the British and turned around, whereupon they were pursued by the 1st Troop under Captain Hornby, and the 4th Troop. Corporal E. Thomas of the 4th opened fire near the chateau of Ghislain, the first British soldier to do so in the Great War. He was uncertain whether he killed or wounded the German soldier that he hit. Meanwhile, Hornby led his men in hot pursuit and charged the Germans, killing several. He returned with his sword presented, revealing German blood.

Meanwhile to the rear, having got an idea that things were about to get a bit heavy, the BEF decided to dig in a loose line along the Mons-Conde canal. They didn't really know how many Germans were on the other side of the canal, but they would find out soon enough. Suffice to say, it would not be a fair fight. Less than 80,000 British troops with 300 odd pieces of artillery, were about to face off against 160,000 German soldiers who were backed up by double the amount of artillery. Ouch!

The BEF had two distinct advantages amongst many challenges. Firstly, they were professional soldiers, highly skilled and probably the best exponents of the noble art of rifle fire on the planet. Secondly, the German 1st Army, whom they were facing, were under strict orders not to risk outflanking the British, thus potentially losing touch with the German 2nd Army, so they had to launch a frontal attack, which they duly did at dawn on 23rd August 1914.

The war was most definitely on.

The German artillery opened up at dawn with the first infantry attack commencing at 9am, their objectives were to take control of the bridges that crossed the canal, once in possession of these bridges they were to push on directly to the British lines and beyond. They advanced across open country in close formation making a perfect target for the trained British riflemen. The result was carnage. The Germans suffered terribly, and by noon the German bodies were piling up all over the place. They had made next to no progress at all.

However, during this time the BEF were being shelled constantly by the massed German artillery and enjoyed little or no cover. Despite this, they held on for six hours before blowing the bridges over the canal and retreating to a pre-established second line position a few miles away. The Germans were tired and disorganised and failed to press home any advantage despite their huge numerical superiority. German reserves were called up and massed for a new attack in the evening. It was here that the British commanders finally realised the size of the enemy, and promptly ordered the retreat. They had already lost 1,600 men and didn't fancy losing too many more. The men were organised, rounded up and the order was given: a fighting retreat towards Maubeuge and then down the road from Bavai to Le Cateau almost twenty miles away.

An Army on the Run: The First Battle of the Marne

Despite the setback at Mons the German army steamrollered through northern France. It seemed to the Kaiser that it would be only a matter of time until he would be enjoying *vin rouge et croissants* in Paris. He sent medals and congratulatory telegrams to his senior officers, but deep down most of these soldiers were worried about the situation. The heroic defensive actions from the BEF at Mons, and again at Le Cateau, along with the dogged resistance of the Belgians had destroyed the careful timing of the Schlieffen Plan. They were also concerned that their armies had been fighting and marching for a month without rest. They had advanced more than 300 miles in that time and their supplies were stretched to the limit. They were tired and questions hung over their ability to land the decisive blow to Paris, if they ever got there.

Likewise the British and French troops were also feeling the pace after enduring more than ten days continual retreat under constant attack from the German guns. They eventually reached a line of relative safety approximately 40 miles south of the River Marne where they finally got a bit of rest. It would be the calm before the storm.

After a scuffle at Guise where the French won a tactical victory, von Bulow, the German Second Army Commander panicked a little and asked von Kluck and his First Army for help. Halting his march to the south west von Kluck turned his Army east, towards Paris itself. This move closed the gap between the two German

Armies and brought von Kluck to the River Marne, some 30 miles east of Paris, by 3rd of September.

French air reconnaissance discovered this turn, and they quickly prepared a counter-attack. On the morning of 6th September the French Sixth Army, under direction from General Joffre, attacked the Germans First Army flank, achieving complete surprise.

An Army such as von Kluck's was organised with its strongest parts facing forwards, so in an effort to counter the surprise attack, he wheeled his army around to face the French head on. By doing this he opened up a gap between him and the German Second Army. If the French and the BEF could infiltrate this gap they would have access to the left flank of the German First Army and the right flank of the German Second army, which, to use a technical term, would be a right result.

Realising their situation, the Germans had no choice but to withdraw to the north. Between the 10th and 12th September they conducted a fighting retreat covering around forty miles of ground until they established a new line on high ground beyond the River Aisne, destroying everything as they went in an effort to slow the Allied pursuit.

Despite their best efforts, the Allies were unable to finish the Germans off. The chasing Allied soldiers were themselves exhausted, they had run out of shells too and to make matters worse the Germans had dug in on high ground which offered good defensive positions. The Battle of the Marne was over. The Germans had been stopped, but at a cost. Almost 250,000 Allied men were killed, wounded or taken prisoner during this first major battle of the war. A war, it was clear, which would definitely not be over by Christmas.

Revenge in the East, but at a Cost: The Battle of Tannenberg

First things first, the 1914 Battle of Tannenberg did not take place at Tannenberg. It actually took place close to Allenstein some 20 miles to the west. It was decided to be called the Battle of Tannenberg after the event by German High Command to pander to national ideology. They wanted to put to bed the original Battle of Tannenberg, fought in 1410 where the Teutonic Knights were beaten by the Poles and Lithuanians. Although this was over 500 years ago (you would have thought they would have got over it after that amount of time), being beaten by a bunch of Slavs still hurt, obviously.

That said, the 1914 Battle of Tannenberg was, for the Germans, an absolute dandy. In just seven days (23rd – 30th August) of fighting they encircled and practically destroyed Russia's Second Army, taking 95,000 prisoners in the process. Not a bad week's work to be honest.

It all started with the Russians deploying two Armies for the invasion of East Prussia and Germany: First Army under General Rennenkampf to the north and Second Army under General Samsonov to the south. The Schlieffen Plan only allowed for Prussia to be garrisoned fairly lightly with a single Army (the German Eighth Army) and they were outnumbered. Big time. Initial Russian victories forced Germany onto the retreat, pushing them back to the Vistula, allowing the advancing Russians to take East Prussia with little effort.

German high command were concerned and brought in Paul von Hindenburg and Erich Ludendorff to sort out the mess. They promptly ordered the retreat to stop and a counter attack to be launched in an effort to stabilise the front – which it did. They then put in place a bold attacking move, originally devised by Colonel Maximilian Hoffmann, which meant moving the bulk of their troops by train from the north to the south to face the Russian Second Army. It was 'eggs in one basket' time for the Germans...

Now, part of the Russian master plan was that the First Army to the north would eventually spin round to the southwest to get closer to the Second Army, providing a formidable force which would bulldoze its way into Germany. However, there were a couple of issues that caused this plan to fail.

Firstly, Rennenkampf and Samsonov didn't get on. Actually they hated each other. Communication was at best frosty and Samsonov had no clue that the First Army had practically stopped and carried on with his plan to cut off the retreating Germans. He pushed the bulk of his men west to encircle the retreating Germans and left a weak force holding a forty mile front to the northeast, which was expected to meet up with the Second Army coming south. Or so he thought.

Actually, the Second Army had had a tougher time of it than expected and had paused to reorganise after a tough scrap at Gumbinnen. They weren't coming to link up with the First Army at all.

Additionally, the Russians had over extended their communications line. They could no longer send encrypted messages, and when the Germans intercepted two messages on

25th August which told them the distance between the two Russian Armies and their relative marching plans, they knew that if they attacked Samsonov in the south, Rennenkampf was too far away to offer any help.

On 27th August the attack was launched on Samsonov's weak north eastern front with immediate success. The border town of Soldau was captured, destroying communication with Samsonov's central force. To capitalise on this success, a mass of German troops were sent from the north to encircle Samsonov's forces. Critically short of supplies, his exhausted troops in disarray and with no safe communication system, Samsonov had no choice but to give the order to retreat on 28th August. However it was too late. By the 29th his forces were surrounded and cut off.

Hindenburg and Ludendorff were lauded as heroes, even though it wasn't really their plan that won. It didn't matter though, what mattered was that Germany had just won a spectacular victory. Out of an estimated 150,000 men at Samsonov's disposal, only 10,000 escaped. The Germans took 95,000 prisoners and 500 pieces of artillery. Samsonov committed suicide.

The news of the Russian defeat was a catastrophe for the Allies, so much so that the decision was made to keep the news away from the British public. But was it as bad as it seemed? The Germans had moved one cavalry division and three corps of infantry (about 85,000 men) away from the Western Front to the East to help beat the Russians. This undoubtedly helped the cause of the French and the British at the Battle of the Marne and the German advance on Paris had been stopped. They may not have known it at the time, but perhaps it was the Russians who had saved Paris?

On Your Marks: The Race to the Sea

After the failure of the German army to press their advantage on the Western Front during the Battle of the Marne, Moltke was shown the door. In his place came a chap called Erich von Falkenhayn. He was full of ambition and wanted to restore the momentum of the initial German advance before the setback at the Marne. To be honest, the last thing he wanted was to stop attacking and order his troops to dig defensive positions all along the line. That wasn't going to win anything.

Falkenhayn continued to eye up Belgium, he still thought he could sneak in round the back and resume the Schlieffen Plan with a swift blow to the north. After the frantic struggles of Mons, Le Cateau, and The Marne there were only minimal numbers of troops from either side positioned north of the River Oise and both sides saw an opportunity to ruin the others supply system. The Germans had an elaborate rail network running in this area supplying troops and animals with vital supplies. To disrupt this supply would severely impact the fighting potential of the German army. Similarly, Falkenhayn also sensed an opportunity; he wanted the Belgian North Sea ports. If he could get control of those then the British supply lines from these areas as well as those in Northern France such as Calais, would be cut off and would force the BEF to look for alternative, more distant supply routes such as from Normandy or Brittany. These were hundreds of miles to the south of where the current action was and would have caused huge supply issues for the British.

The Royal Navy also had their eyes on these ports, but for different reasons. They were worried that if the Germans captured them the German High Seas Fleet, especially the U-boats, would pose a serious threat to the Royal Navy's control of the North Sea. They were also worried that the enemy would be getting close enough to bombard Britain from the sea, this would not do, and as such they urged the army to move swiftly north to gain the ports.

Therefore all sides had good reason to stretch their lines to the west and north. Their plans were almost identical – hoping to turn each other's flanks in an effort to disrupt supply networks. This series of out-flanking manoeuvres became known as the race to the sea. The name was somewhat ironic as it was neither a race, nor was the sea the main goal of either side. But it sold papers and books, so that was ok.

So, from September until November each army had a go at out-flanking the other, only to run headlong into each other. Like a bee trying to fly through a window this pattern continued until they literally ran out of dry land.

By the end of 1914 this so called race to the sea had ended in a draw. Two continuous lines of trenches had developed, stretching from the Belgian coast to the Swiss border. Mobile war had had its chance and had not come up with the goods, now there were no flanks to turn and no space to exploit. Instead the war would become less mobile and much more direct.

Welcome to the age of trench warfare.

An Army Destroyed: First Ypres

As the race to the sea continued apace, both sides had an eye on the Belgian town of Ypres (pronounced 'ee-preh' but known as 'Wipers' to many British soldiers). The British liked it because of its good transport links and close proximity to the critical channel ports; it was a natural hub for new arrivals and supplies from Britain. On the other hand, the Germans saw Ypres as the gateway to the rest of Belgium and beyond. Its proximity to the coast would mean they could push on and gain control of the ports and put the British under server logistical pressure.

On 1st October the BEF began to filter their troops away from the flanking movements of the race to the sea and moved them north towards Ypres. At the same time, what was left of the Belgian Army had assembled to the north at Dixmunde, along the banks of the Yser River. They all dug in, rested as best they could, and waited further instructions. It was all about to kick off big style. The Germans wanted Ypres, badly, so badly in fact that they called up huge numbers of re-enforcements into the area. Little did they know it, but the Belgians were facing over 40,000 Germans who meant business. The odds were not looking good for the Allies.

After assessing the situation, French General Ferdinand Foch decided to attack. He hoped for a repeat of the Battle of the Marne where a surprise offensive would knock the enemy back onto the defensive. There was even talk of pushing on deep into Belgium and onto Lille, but that was a little far-fetched. Having said that, there were some successes in this attack and the optimistic generals urged the troops on and on... but with German re-enforcements and artillery arriving every day, the exhausted troops had ran out of puff by the 20th October.

Meanwhile, on that same day (20th) the Germans went for it with two simultaneous attacks: One directly against the Belgians at Dixmunde and the other straight at Ypres itself. The attack at Dixmunde was swift and powerful, and posed a real threat to the channel ports. On 22nd October, the German infantry, made up of volunteers and new draftees, some reportedly only 16 years of age, attacked the British at Bixschoote, singing as they advanced over open ground straight into British rifle and machine gun fire. They were cut to pieces, with many battalions suffering up to 70% casualties. Stories of these young men singing as they marched to their death became the stuff of legend on both sides of the line, and were used extensively by Nazi propagandists twenty years later. But, somehow, despite the men being at the limits of physical and mental endurance, the line held long enough for the decision to be made, on 27th October, for the sluice gates that kept the North Sea out of Flanders to be opened.

Once opened the water levels in Flanders rose and provided a belt of marsh land twenty miles long and two miles wide that protected the Allies from the German invaders who were no longer able to move their troops and heavy equipment across the water and mud. The attack around Dixmunde floundered and came to a stop. Ypres, on the other hand, had not flooded and was still there for the taking. The Germans renewed their attacks on the 31st October and immediately drove British cavalry from Messines Ridge. The British line, Ypres, and indeed the fate of the war hung by a thread. However, with defeat seeming inevitable, the British launched a desperate counter attack and recovered some of the lost ground, but surely it was just a matter of time before Ypres was in German hands?

This is certainly what the Germans themselves thought, and Kaiser Wilhelm II arrived at the front in anticipation of leading his troops through the town in a victory march. On the 11th November the elite Prussian Guards threw themselves at Ypres, backed by the heaviest artillery bombardment witnessed so far on the Western Front. British cooks, orderlies, and other support staff picked up rifles and bayonets and threw back the attackers. The line held.

Casualties had been horrific (approximately 54,000 British, 50,000 French, and 19,000 Belgian casualties); in addition the German casualty figure is believed to be in excess of 100,000 men. The fighting around Ypres between 14th October and 22nd November effectively destroyed the BEF as a legitimate fighting force.

But Ypres had been saved.

Merry Christmas Fritz! The 1914 Truce

By the end of the year it was apparent that this would be a war fought differently to those before. It would be a war with no glamour or glory, but one of grit and determination. It was a war where the science of defence had grossly out-paced the science of attack; modern weapons meant there would be no more swash-buckling cavalry advance, no more mobile tactics. Instead it was dig, dig, dig, and keep your head down. The trenches of 1914 were rudimentary at best. Neither side were expecting a long drawn out war, as a consequence no one really put too much time and effort into constructing habitable lines. The cold and wet weather didn't help much either. Many soldiers were ill equipped for winter, with supplies of coats and woollen clothes slow to reach the front lines. As the winter rain continued to fall the soldiers got very cold, very damp, and very miserable. Their mood was not helped much by their surroundings turning from mud to slime. Movement was difficult and supplies from the rear were either very delayed or didn't make it at all. The enthusiasm of those early weeks of war had disappeared for good.

It was in this environment that an attitude of improvisation and survival prevailed. In these early months of war, the men in the trenches established their own code of behaviour towards the enemy. An unwritten rule of 'live and let live' was followed by both sides, culminating in the widespread (but not complete) truce of Christmas 1914.

Inspired by this kindly attitude, as well as a natural longing to relax a little at this time of year, the truce was also definitely helped by the weather. The dull, wet and damp weather had been replaced on Christmas Eve with clear, sharp, crisp air and a strong frost, which definitely added to the festive feelings.

It all started on the 24th, the day that the Germans traditionally celebrated Christmas. They decorated their trenches with candles and sang hymns. In many places, where the opposing trench lines were only a matter of metres apart, the British could hear the singing and joined in with their own songs. The evening hours were passed as each side sang to the other and shouted out 'Merry Christmas Tommy!' and 'Merry Christmas Fritz' from the trenches.

Eventually one or two soldiers tentatively shouted out to the other side to meet in No Man's Land. This was obviously a risk, but as one, then two, soldiers climbed over the parapet without a shot being fired, more men followed. Soon, up and down the front there was a spontaneous meeting of soldiers in the morass of the battlefield. Swapping photos, badges, and buttons, swapping cigars for bully beef, and cigarettes for chocolates. It was all very friendly and not one single shot was fired in anger. In some places football matches were played, and although there is no real evidence available as to who won, it is most probable that the Germans won. On penalties!

As Christmas Day drew to a close, the rain started to fall on the Western Front once more as if it was a sign that that the truce was over and it was time to get back to the war; back to the mud; back to the guns.

The French Get Stuck In: The First Champagne Offensive

There was no such Christmas truce in the Champagne area of the Western Front. Here both sides had been at each other's throats since the middle of December. It was this part of the front, situated roughly between Reims and Verdun, which the French High Command had chosen for a big offensive. They had picked this specific area for two reasons really; this area was directly to the south of a large salient (bulge in the line) that meant the Germans were only 70miles from Paris, which understandably made the French a bit nervous. Secondly, directly behind this line were important regions of natural resources such as coal and iron ore which would be needed if the war dragged on.

Ever the optimist, the French Commander-in-Chief, Joseph Joffre, was still convinced (despite the failure of previous attacks on entrenched positions) that a full on infantry attack would succeed, and that his armies would break through the German lines and march on to a swift and decisive victory. His plan was simple. Amass a huge number of infantry, backed up by an equally impressive line of guns and hope that sheer numbers win the day. The attack was planned for both the north and the south edges of the salient, followed by a drive north through the Ardennes to cut off the fleeing Germans.

The problem here was that the majority of the French guns were 75mm pieces which were great for open, mobile warfare but not that great at cutting enemy barbed wire or flattening concrete defences. They also couldn't cope with the rate of fire that was needed for the offensive and often broke down. Add to this the fact that the Germans had nice strong defensive positions on high ground with good visibility and it was no surprise that things didn't go according to plan.

The opening attacks rushed forward near Perthes in eastern Champagne, on 10th December. This was quickly followed by five days of heavy fighting around Givenchy between 18th and 22nd December and another battle for Perthes on the 20th. All failed to deliver the breakthrough, in fact the gains they had achieved were barely noticeable. The French had another go on 22nd December, this time at Noyon, but again came up against efficiently entrenched German defences. They were particularly effective with the machine gun which tore the attacking French infantry to pieces time and time again. In just over two weeks of fighting the French had taken 30,000 casualties for minimal territorial gain.

The losses didn't deter Joffre, although he did warn the French government not to expect any sudden victories. He planned another large attack in exactly the same place as the others had failed in an effort to cut off the German railway links four miles behind enemy lines. This was a huge ask considering the results of the previous attack, unless there were to be some significant changes in tactics or a new master strategy.

Unfortunately, there were no changes in tactics, and no new strategy; just more men and more guns. The advance took place on 16th February (delayed for four days due to snowstorms), which gave the Germans more time to prepare their defences. Along an eight mile front, no French soldier was able to advance more than 1,500m.

By the time the attacks were mercifully called off on 17th March the French army had suffered 94,342 casualties to gain less than 1 square mile of smashed French farmland.

Merde.

Tag-Team War: Neuve Chapelle

In early 1915 the Western Front resembled a tag-team wrestling match. No sooner had the French had jumped out of the ring after the disaster of Champagne, they slapped the hand of the British who took up the baton for the Allies and launched their own offensive at Neuve Chapelle.

The objective handed to the British First Army, led by Field Marshal Douglas Haig, was to take the village of Neuve Chapelle and then gain control of Aubers Ridge; a ridge of higher ground less than a mile to the east of the village that offered a commanding view of the surrounding area and would be an ideal launching pad for an advance towards German held Lille. This was to be the first time the British had launched an attack on their own, and it was about time too. During the previous eight months they had retreated, counter-attacked, marched, dug trenches by the mile and fought a defensive war, now, at last, the British Tommies would be able to give Fritz an absolute hiding. Or at least that was the plan.

This was a new kind of war, a static war of attrition rather than fluid movements in the open that the British Army was more used to. However, Haig and his staff got their head around the issues of planning for a full-on attack quite well. Aerial reconnaissance provided intelligence of the size, position and depth of enemy defences. Meticulous time tables were drawn up for the artillery guns; they even built a light railway to ensure supplies could be brought to the front in a timely manner.

At 7.30am on 10th March, the guns let rip. First off it was 35 minutes of hellfire directly onto the German front line. Haig wanted the bombardment to be much longer, by a shortage of shells forced his hand. However, in those thirty-five minutes the British guns fired more shells than in the entire South African war of 1899-1902. At 8.05am the guns lifted and the infantry of the British First Army (including a large number of Indian troops) advanced along a two mile front. The guns then switched their attack to the village of Neuve Chapelle itself, and the rear of the German lines, in an effort to deter re-enforcements and supplies to the front.

Maybe it was the organisation of the advancing infantry, maybe it was the fact that this part of the front was only lightly defended by the Germans, maybe the short preliminary bombardment didn't raise the alarm that an attack was imminent. Whatever the reason (and it was probably a mixture of all three mentioned above), what followed next was a rare, rare bird indeed: a genuine and bona fide breakthrough of the enemy lines. By 8.30am Allied troops had captured the village of Neuve Chapelle. Get In!

However, it was not all tea and cupcakes. There was a small part of the German line, situated nearest the ridge, which had not been bombarded at all; the guns didn't get up to the line quick enough to take part in the attack. The German wire was untouched, the hostile machine gun placements were not damaged, the enemy troops were still there. The Indian soldiers who advanced on this sector in three successive waves stood no chance. Communications were so bad though that because no one returned back to their lines in this sector, HQ thought they had succeeded in their objective. The grisly fact was they had all been killed or wounded; the best part of a thousand men were cut to pieces in a matter of minutes.

Once the main breakthrough had been achieved the successful attackers succumbed to a number of communication and supply issues that would blight both sides continually until the end of the war. Haig found it difficult, if not impossible, to keep in contact with his field commanders. As a consequence opportunities to advance were missed due to a lack of concrete orders. Many field commanders, inexperienced with this kind of war, hampered by limited or no communications were unwilling to send their units forward without proper support and decided to err on the side of caution. Instead of pushing east towards Lille as originally planned, they stopped and consolidated to take a breath and get prepared to meet whatever German counter-attack would appear.

That counter-attack didn't appear, and on the morning of 11th March the British attacked once more. This time, however, the Germans were expecting them and the advancing infantry suffered terribly from machine-gun and artillery fire. In many areas the reserve troops could not even get to the front line due to German artillery fire to the rear of the British lines. Despite continued attempts, the British failed to take any more ground. Nonetheless, Haig ordered preparations to be made for a resumed offensive the next morning. Oh joy.

The Germans, however, had their own plan. Having soaked up two days of continual British attacks now it was their turn to have a go. On the morning of 12th March more than 10,000 German soldiers launched a counter-attack. Unfortunately for the Germans, their attacks were just as dis-organised as the British and although they recovered some ground, the British had held on to Neuve Chapelle. Just. But it didn't come cheap; this three day battle had cost the Allies 11,600 men killed, missing or wounded.

Bully Beef and Rats: Life in the Trenches

It is impossible for any modern day individual to really understand what it was like in the trenches of WW1. The nearest we can get would be to dig a dirty great big hole in our garden and live it in for a week, limiting ourselves to one tin of corned beef and one cup of water a day, and then invite our neighbours and friends to hose us down with a hosepipe every now and again and randomly throw live grenades at us. It was an insane mixture of tedious monotony punctuated by moments of sheer terror. Sounds like a perfect way to spend a summer week. Not.

The regular routine of trench life involved a monotonous existence of bad food, bad smells and even worse conditions. Hot food was generally banned from the front line trenches in case steam or smoke revealed their locations. Food for the front line troops was either pre-prepared cold fare (in tins, cans or jars) or was prepared remotely by mobile field kitchens and sent to the front lines. By the time it arrived it was often cold and not particularly tasty.

Typically any given Battalion would serve a spell in the front line, then spend some time in the support lines, then in reserve and then they would be allowed a short period of rest, before returning to the front line again for the cycle to begin once more. A typical day in the front line trenches started before dawn with 'Stand To'. Everyone in the trenches were woken up and ordered to fix bayonets and climb on to the fire step to ward off any enemy dawn raid. Both sides practised this 'Stand To' procedure religiously up and down the line, and they both knew that each other did this. Yet, still dawn raids occurred. To make doubly sure there were no enemy troops lurking in the dawn mist often machine guns, rifles and some artillery were fired indiscriminately into No Man's Land.

After 'Stand To' it was breakfast and weapon cleaning time. Breakfast often consisted of bully beef or other tinned fare and would be brought up in containers from the field kitchens behind the lines. In some areas rum was issued to warm up the troops after a cold night in the trenches. Weapon cleaning was done in shifts, with only a portion of the men cleaning their weapons at any one time.

With breakfast over there was a quick inspection by the Commanding Officer and then it was down to work. The trenches didn't look after themselves and there were always lots of improvements and repairs needed: repairing duckboards, refilling sandbags, draining water from the trench, repairing and reinforcing the walls of the trench were just some of the exciting tasks that were waiting for the average British Tommy in the trenches. During the day such work was restricted to bits that could be done within the relative safety of the trench. With snipers continuously monitoring the front line, popping your head above the parapet was pretty dangerous. In fact, you probably only ever did that once.

With work over, Tommy could relax a little. Many soldiers would take advantage of quiet periods to snatch a bit of sleep or write some letters home.

As the light faded it was time to 'Stand To' again in case the enemy decided to launch a raid in the murky light of dusk. It was only when it was dark that the real action began. Most of the work needed in repairing and maintain the trenches were carried out at night. Rations and water would also be brought up from reserve. Then there was sentry duty; standing on the fire step keeping an eye/ear out for any enemy movement in No Man's Land. Sentry duty was limited to two hours to stop soldiers falling asleep on duty, something which was punishable by death.

Some of the most dangerous jobs on the front line meant going out into No Man's Land. Being out there a soldier felt very exposed, the slightest sound would alert the enemy and the whole area would erupt in a fury of flares and machine guns. With little or no cover, and a nervous enemy ready to over-react to the slightest noise, No Man's Land was a truly deadly place to be. However, patrols had to get out there to repair barbed wire, check on enemy movements, and recover equipment as well as dead or wounded colleagues.

Indeed, death was a constant companion to the soldiers in the front line. Even when there was no major action there was always 'natural wastage' as the staff officers, positioned miles behind the lines would crassly call it. Snipers were all too happy to oblige if any soldier tried to peer over the parapet, then there was the shelling of the lines, which was a constant irritant.

Another reason for 'natural wastage' was disease. Rats and lice infested the trenches in their millions. Drawn to them by all the dead bodies, rats were absolutely everywhere and they were despised by soldiers on both sides. They tried everything to get rid of them, officers would offer prizes to the men who killed the most, but nothing they did made any difference.

Welcome to the world of the front line trench. There is no place like home.

Going Undergound: Hill 60 (1915)

Hill 60 was a man-made hill born from the spoil thrown up during the construction of a railway line. It was situated towards the south of the Ypres salient on the Western Front and dominated the surrounding flat landscape of Flanders. Ypres was a few miles to the north, and if you stood on Hill 60 in 1915 you could still see the towers of the Cloth Hall as they hadn't yet been blown to bits. Therefore, this man made pile of Flanders mud was strategically vital for both sides and would be the scene of intense and bitter fighting for a number of years.

The Germans had wrenched the hill from the French in December 1914, and when the British had replaced them in this sector they set about making plans to get it back. Whilst making these plans someone had the splendid idea of digging tunnels beneath the hill, depositing a shed load of explosives in the tunnels, standing well back and blowing the hill off the face of the planet. 'Bravo!' said the British Commanders and the digging started in earnest in January 1915 by the 171st Tunnelling Company of the Royal Engineers.

By 10th April everything was set. All tunnels were dug and the six mines were ready to be charged. The Germans had no clue they were sitting directly on top of as-near-as-makes-no-difference 10,000lbs of explosives. Zero hour was set: 17th April at 7pm.

The mines detonated perfectly, sending tonnes of Flanders mud, sandbags, trench timbers, and broken German bodies hundreds of feet in the air. Before this lot had fallen back down to earth every British available gun opened up and poured shrapnel over the

German lines. Almost immediately afterwards, the British infantry rushed forwards towards what was left of the German defensive lines. They met little resistance and completely over-ran the enemy with the loss of only seven attackers.

However, celebrations were cut short. That night the Germans launched one hell of a counter attack and kicked the British off what was left of the hill. Twenty-four hours later, thanks to heroic work by the 2nd Duke of Wellington's and the 2nd King's Own Yorkshire Light Infantry Hill 60 was back in British hands.

Over the next few days the fighting was particularly vicious, the Germans really wanted that hill back. During a particularly insistent attempt by the Germans to re-take the Hill on the night of 20th/21st April, four British soldiers won the Victoria Cross, The Empire's highest award for gallantry. Those soldiers were Edward Dwyer (East Surrey Regiment), Benjamin Geary (East Surrey Regiment), George Roupell (East Surrey Regiment) and Geoffrey Woolley (Queen Victoria Rifles).

Hill 60 remained in the hands of the British.

There is Something in the Air: The First Large Scale Gas Attack

Those troops that were forced from Hill 60 after the first German counter-attack were broken, but not due to exhaustion and battle fatigue as you would expect. They ran back to their lines coughing, chocking, and gasping for air. They were convinced they had been gassed. And they were right, but it was not intentional.

OK, the French were actually the first people to use gas in WW1 (In August 1914 they threw tear gas grenades at the Germans), and both sides were looking to science to break the deadlock of trench warfare, but it was the Germans that got their heads around large scale gas attacks first, which is why they are the subject of this chapter. And they weren't using tear gas either. No, that wasn't hardcore enough; their gas of choice was chlorine. Instead of being a bit of a nuisance and stinging your eyes, this stuff would cause enemy soldiers to drown in their own blood if they breathed in enough of it. Yes, that was much more like it.

By early 1915 the Germans had been playing with gas for a while, but they were not quite ready. That said, they had dug some gas cylinders into the side of Hill 60, and during the frantic artillery shoot-out a couple of the cylinders had cracked and leaked out a small amount of their cruel contents. The trouble was, with all what was going on it was not possible to differentiate small clouds of chlorine gas from the clouds of dust, the fumes and mud of each artillery explosion, not to mention the dirty great big mines that were detonated.

By April 1915 they were ready. Everything was set. The plan was to launch a major offensive in the Ypres sector, but the wind direction was critical for the successful deployment of gas. They waited for a south-westerly breeze to appear. They waited. And waited. The weeks went past and the wind stubbornly persisted in a northerly direction. The German High Command were getting a little 'windy' themselves. The longer they waited around the more people knew about their little ruse and the bigger the chance they would be rumbled before they had even started.

Maybe they started doing some weird 'wind-dance', because during the afternoon of 22nd April the wind changed. This was it! The German guns opened up on the enemy front – held by Canadians and French Algerians. Once the bombardment had stopped, the men of the aptly nick-named 'Stinkpionere' donned their masks and opened the cylinders. When the Allied troops had crawled back into their trenches after the guns had gone quiet they readied themselves for the advancing infantry. That was what always happened right? Guns, guns guns, guns. Stop. Quiet. Infantry advance. Fight for your life. Those were just the rules. Only this time, the rules were different. There were no enemy soldiers, just a wall of yellow-green smoke that slowly drifted towards them.

The effects were devastating. All along the affected line soldiers coughed, choked, threw up violently and generally panicked. Men were dropping like flies, not by bullets, but by something invisible and sinister. It was new, it was mysterious and it scared the living daylights out of the troops. Those that were not affected by the gas simply ran, leaving a huge hole in the line four miles wide. Fifteen minutes after the release of the gas the awaiting German infantry donned their masks and advanced. They were ready for a fight, as was normal in these kind of attacks, but when they reached the enemy lines there was no one there. Within the hour they had advance more than a mile with hardly a shot fired. The war was as good as won, wasn't it?

Thing was, the Germans were not really prepared for such a sudden and dramatic opportunity. The cavalry were miles behind the lines, and there were no real infantry reserves in position. By the time they had organised themselves the French had got themselves together again and had once more formed a decent defensive line. The opportunity had been lost.

The German's Attack: Second Ypres

The German gas attack of 22nd April signalled the start of the Second Battle of Ypres. A German offensive was a rare occurrence on the Western Front. The reasons behind this particular one were twofold: to test the impact of gas in warfare and to distract attention from the mass movement of troops away from the Western Front towards the East to fight the Russians.

The result of the first gas attack was a large French/Algerian sized hole in the Allied defensive line. This was quickly plugged with Canadian troops who fought valiantly to steady the line in the face of intense artillery and infantry assaults.

A second full on gas attack was thrown at the Canadians on the 24th. The Canadians had no breathing equipment and were forced to evacuate the first line of trenches. However, Canadian artillery fired shrapnel shells over open sights to keep the German infantry from taking their positions. Another hindrance for the Germans was the lack of their own artillery support due to poor visibility through the gas cloud, without any enemy artillery to bother them, Canadian soldiers in the second line trenches were free to fire at the assaulting enemy troops and beat off the attacks, inflicting heavy casualties in doing so.

The fighting on the 24th was fierce and wide reaching, spreading as far as Hill 60 to the south. Outnumbered, out-gunned and out-gassed, even with British re-enforcements, it was obvious to the Second Army Commander, General Smith-Dorrien, that the current line was untenable. He requested a fighting retreat to a line closer to Ypres that would allow a more effective defence. His

Commander-in-Chief (Sir John French) responded to this request by sending him home, replacing him with General Plumer.

However, it didn't take Plumer long to realise that Smith-Dorrien was right, a tactical reverse was needed. Strangely French accepted Plumer's request, but asked him to delay to see what the result of a French counterattack in the region would bring about. Two French Divisions attacked on 29th September and failed miserably; the retreat was ordered on 1st May.

The Germans launched another attack at Ypres, but were again beaten back by stubborn Allied resistance, despite them taking large numbers of casualties. The fighting continued throughout May. It was often vicious with no quarter given on either side. By the end of the month the battle drew to a close due to a lack of ammunition and manpower on both sides.

The Germans had succeeded in pushing forward several miles across a large part of the Ypres salient, creeping ever closer to the city. But at what cost? Germany had lost 35,000 dead and wounded, Britain and the Empire had lost 60,000, France 10,000 and Belgium 1,500.

Frustrated at not taking Ypres, the Germans decided to knock seven bells out of the city over the coming months, gradually reducing the once magnificent cloth hall and other imposing structures to a pile of bricks.

But Ypres was held. Again.

We Need More Men: Kitchener's New Army

Field Marshall Earl Kitchener of Khartoum became Minster of War on August 5th 1914 and immediately put in place plans to greatly expand the British Army. Unlike the majority of people of the time, he did not think that the war would be over by Christmas, instead he foresaw a long, drawn out conflict that would require a lot more men than the BEF currently had.

He didn't fancy using the Territorial Army as a basis to expand British military presence as members of the Territorials could opt to avoid overseas service, and, in his opinion, Britain didn't need a big home service army, she needed men on the Western Front, giving Fritz what for. So he decided to expand the regular army by raising a new version of wartime volunteers aged between 19 and 30 who would agree to sign up for the duration of the war and importantly, would agree to be sent anywhere the army needed them.

On the 6th August parliament agreed to an increase of 500,000 men of all ranks.

The call went out to the men of Great Britain: Your King and Country needs you. General Sir Henry Rawlinson wondered if men would be more inclined to enlist in the Army if they knew they would serve alongside their mates. To test his theory, he appealed to London stockbrokers to raise a battalion of men from workers in the City of London. A week later 1,600 men had enlisted in the 10th (Service) Battalion, Royal Fusiliers, the so-called "Stockbrokers' Battalion."

A few days later, Edward Stanley, the 17th Earl of Derby, decided to follow this example and organised the formation of a battalion of men from Liverpool. Within two days 1,500 Scousers had joined the new battalion. Speaking to these men Lord Derby said: "This should be a battalion of pals, a battalion in which friends from the same office will fight shoulder to shoulder for the honour of Britain and the credit of Liverpool." Within the next few days three more battalions were raised in Liverpool.

The country had listened, two weeks after Kitchener's Call to Arms the first 100,000 men had signed up. Kitchener had his first Army (named 'K1') made up of six Divisions. On 28th August Kitchener asked for another 100,000 men. To help the recruitment effort the idea of the Pals Battlaions were promoted heavily up and down the country; also the age limits were widened to thirty-five for men with no experience, forty-five for ex-soldiers and fifty for old Non Commissioned Officers (NCO's).

By the end of September 1914, over fifty towns had formed one or more Pals Battalions and there were enough men for another army ('K2'). Three more Armies were sanctioned by the War Office by October. All together a total of thirty new Divisions (in 1915 a single Division included about 19,500 men) were in the process of being built. It was, quite simply, an incredible achievement.

In March 1915 an order was issued to create a sixth Army. By the end of December 1915 many original regular battalions had a large contingent of volunteers who had replaced the losses of the previous eighteen months of fighting.

So, the men were in place, but what about the weapons, uniforms, medical centres, accommodation, vehicles, animals, ammunition, guns, training centres, experienced officers and commanders needed to transform these men into a professional and effective fighting unit?

In reality, no regiment had the required amount of equipment for the new intake. Many men trained in their own clothes, some regiments dug out old uniforms dating from earlier wars for recruits (or at least NCO's) to wear. With regards to guns, there weren't many of those around either. All of the available artillery was already at the front, and many regiments had to make do with wooden replica rifles for training purposes.

By spring 1915 many of these issues had been overcome and Kitchener's Armies trained hard. Training this lot was tough. Few of the volunteers had any soldiering experience and the majority had never held a rifle, let alone fired an artillery piece or a machine gun. The progress was slow, and British Commanders were not convinced that these Armies would perform very well on the Western Front.

Time would tell if they were correct. The first battalions would see fighting on the Western Front around the town of Loos in just a few months' time. The rest would have to wait until 1916 and the 'Big Push' on the Somme to get a piece of the action.

Six VC's Before Breakfast: The Gallipoli Landings

At the same time as the French and British infantry were being subjected to gas attacks on the Western Front, the Allied seaborne landings on the Gallipoli peninsular (now named Gelibolu in modern day Turkey) were taking place. The date was 25th April 1915.

The reasons behind an attack in this region were numerous; The Allies were keen to open up an effective supply route to Russia; the fighting in Europe had blocked the natural land based trade routes to the west and the Baltic Sea routes were blocked by the German Navy. The only other route that could be used was via the Mediterranean and Black Seas, the latter was controlled by the Ottoman (or Turkish) Empire. If the Dardanelles that connected the Black Sea to the Mediterranean could be captured, the route to Russia would be secured. Secondly, with stalemate on the Western Front, the Allies were looking around for other ways of kick starting their war effort. They thought that by dragging the Ottomans into the war, it might draw Bulgaria and Greece into the ring on the side of the Allies.

On 19th February the French and British Navies tried to force the Dardanelle Straights by smashing the coastal defences and forts to smithereens. An intercepted message suggested that coastal forts were running out of ammunition, surely the Straight was there for the taking? The main attack was planned for 18th March. At the head of the fleet the minesweepers came under intense fire from the coastal defences. Many of these minesweepers were manned by civilians, and they soon had had enough and turned around, leaving the minefields mostly intact. As the rest of the fleet continued on their way they ran straight into a rather large mine field. Numerous Allied ships, including HMS Irresistible, HMS Inflexible, and HMS Ocean were sunk. The losses forced the Allies to halt the naval campaign, if the Dardanelles were to be captured ground forces were going to be needed to be landed on the peninsula. It would be another 6 weeks before the troops arrived in earnest to hop ashore. This delay gave the Ottoman forces time to prepare defences and get in reinforcements.

The landings were pencilled in for 25th April and were to take place in two different locations: Cape Helles and Ari Burnu. On the day of the landings, Cape Helles saw 35,000 Anglo-French troops clamber ashore at five distinct areas ('Y', 'X', 'W', 'V', and 'S' beaches). Ten miles up the coast 17,000 ANZACS (members of the Australian and New Zealand Army Corps) were making a b-line for 'Z' beach at Ari Burnu. In truth, they should have been a mile further south at Gaba Tepe, which would have been a much easier place to advance from, but for some reason, possibly a navigation error, they ended up at Ari Burnu, a much smaller cape which was surrounded by steep cliffs.

That said, the ANZACS had managed to get 8,000 men ashore by 8am and began to push forward up steep terrain in an attempt to capture the higher ground. By now, the Turkish defenders were concentrating heavy rifle fire onto the ANZACS and inflicting significant casualties. Fanatical counter attacks by the Turks held the Australians back, they could only get two-thirds of the way up the slope towards the plateau. By nightfall both sides were exhausted. With retreat impossible, the ANZACS had no choice but to dig in as best they could and prepare themselves to tough it out.

Meanwhile, further south, the Anglo-French landings, overseen by General Sir Ian Hamilton enjoyed mixed fortunes. At 'Y' beach, 3,000 men were ashore, unopposed, by 6am. A similar situation greeted the slightly smaller contingent who landed ashore at 'S' beach. On 'X' beach the intimidating garrison of twelve Turkish defenders surrendered immediately and the attackers reached the cliff top without a single casualty. They then quickly turned towards 'W' beach where things were not going according to plan.

At 'W' beach the naval bombardment that had preceded the landings had failed to cut the underwater barbed wire or destroy much of the defence system around the beach. A small number of Turks were waiting for the troops when they landed. They waited in silence, fingers on the triggers of their machine guns. 950 men of the Lancashire Fusiliers were sent towards that beach, by the time the beach was secured 260 had been killed and another 283 had been wounded. Six Victoria Crosses were awarded that morning. 'Six VC's before breakfast' is a motto repeated with pride by the fighting men of Lancashire, and 'W' beach is now known as Lancashire Landing.

At 'V' beach things were equally chaotic. The plan here was to use an armoured troop ship, the *River Clyde*, to take 2,000 men right into the shore, whilst another 1,000 men approached the beach in naval cutters, (small wooden boats with oars). Hidden defenders held their fire until the last second and then let rip as the soldiers rushed from the *River Clyde*. The result was utter slaughter. The cutters didn't escape either, these fell under a hail of machine gun and artillery fire and were literally blown to pieces, with many men falling into the water and drowning due to the weight of their kit. So many men were lost in the first hour that a halt to the landings was ordered. They would try again under cover of darkness when the *River Clyde* would attempt to put the remaining troops ashore. By the time the beachhead had been secured, the assaulting troops had lost over half their men. Another six Victoria Crosses were awarded on the beach that day.

As the different beachheads eventually linked up, it seemed that, despite the slaughter on 'V' and 'W' beaches, the overall plan might just work out. There was an opportunity to re-calibrate the main point of the attack to 'Y' beach where the troops had encountered little resistance and were eagerly awaiting further orders to advance. Unfortunately this opportunity was passed over by British Command. They also refused to believe prisoner reports that there were only a few thousand Turkish defenders at Helles. Instead of pushing forward and taking the initiative the attackers chose to consolidate, and wait. Once more an opportunity had been lost.

By nightfall on the 26th there were more than 30,000 Allied troops ashore however the Turkish troops were allowed to retire unmolested to a new line south of Krithia. By the time the Allies were ready for an attack on the 28th, the Turks had reinforced their numbers to match those of the attackers. Stalemate ensued.

Snatching Stalemate from the Jaws of Victory: Sulva Bay

It didn't take a genius to figure out that the landings at Gallipoli had not gone according to plan. Despite several frantic attempts by the Allies to strike out north from Cape Helles the troops were stuck, each attempted advance only achieved to add to the piles of dead bodies that littered the landscape. At Ari Burnu (soon to be renamed ANZAC Cove) they didn't even attempt to breakout. Such were the precarious positions that were held, coupled with a lack of men and supplies that it was deemed best to stay put and wait for reinforcements.

Those reinforcements were on their way. Plans for a new offensive were decided on 7th June 1915. It was an ambitious plan consisting of three simultaneous offensives to achieve a decisive victory. The forces currently holding Cape Helles, despite being exhausted, were to conduct a holding attack, meanwhile the ANZACS, who up until now had hardly advanced a metre since their initial landing, were to somehow magic up a break out of ANZAC Cove and seize the Sari Bair Ridge. They were to get 25,000 fresh reinforcements, but even so this was nothing but optimistic. Both attacks were planned to tie up as many Turkish troops as possible, giving the reserve troops landing at Sulva Bay an easier landing.

With Turkish troops occupied elsewhere, Sulva should have been lightly defended, and the plan there was to get the troops to advance as quickly as possible and link up with the Anzacs. This would conjure up a large front made up of the best part of 60,000 troops which could cut off the southern peninsular and secure the Dardanelles Straight. Easy.

The man in charge of putting all this together was a bit of an odd choice. Lieutenant-General Sir Frederick Stopford was rapidly approaching retirement, had seen very little combat action himself and had never, ever commanded men in battle. Way before the men landed on the beaches, the grey clouds of failure were already gathering rapidly over this critical offensive.

When the landings kicked off just before 10pm on 6th August there were 20,000 Allied troops going ashore against 1,500 defenders. Not surprisingly then, the troops got ashore by the following morning without too much of an issue. Apart from steady sniping in the area there were no major attempts to push the attackers off of the beach.

Remarkably, no instructions were given by Stopford to advance inland. He instead waited until the evening before giving the orders to take the hills immediately inland. Over awkward terrain, in the pitch black, this was easier said than done. The hills were eventually taken but at a cost of 1,700 men. This was the only advance of the day and it had alerted the Turks who quickly set about sending five Divisions to defend Sulva. In reality the Turkish commanders thought they would arrive too late to save the situation. They would be pleasantly surprised.

Stopford, who had been watching the landings from a battleship anchored offshore, was actually very happy with his first day's work. He had no intention of advancing and instead prepared to consolidate. Throughout the 8th August his troops rested. The window of opportunity was rapidly slamming shut.

Belatedly, and only after some prodding by General Sir Ian Hamilton, the Commander of the Allied Mediterranean Expeditionary Force, Stopford ordered his troops to advance on 9th August. The forward troops were made to march two and a half miles to the Tekke Tepe ridge. The march was really tough, over poor terrain and they didn't get near to the summit until 4am on 9th August. Unfortunately for these soldiers, the Turks had beaten them to it and were waiting for them. As the exhausted British troops reached the ridge they were charged with bayonets and practically annihilated. Those that did survive fled back to the beach.

Over the next three days the British tried repeatedly to take the ridge, all of which ended in failure. It was not going well.

Having miraculously snatched bloody stalemate from the jaws of victory, Stopford was shown the door and replaced by General de Lisle on 15th August. Despite inheriting an awful situation, the line was restructured and strengthened and new fighting concentrated on trying to join up Sulva Bay and ANZAC Cove which were no more than 3 miles apart. The continued fighting came to a head on 21st August with the Battle of Scimitar Hill. It was another failure that gained nothing but cost 5,000 Allied lives, many of whom were burned as artillery rounds set fire to the dry vegetation.

Since early August the Allies had suffered 40,000 deaths. When Hamilton asked for another 95,000 men as reinforcements but was only offered 25,000 more large scale attacks in this area were effectively ended.

The situation was complicated more when Bulgaria entered the war on the side of Germany. This meant that another front was needed in the area in Salonika, which would need resources that should have gone to Gallipoli. Also, Germany now had a direct land route to the Ottoman Empire which meant more supplies, more men and more guns could be transferred to the area at a quicker rate. After a personal reconnaissance of the situation by Lord Kitchener, the order to evacuate the peninsular was given.

Between 10th and 20th December the evacuation of 105,000 men and 300 guns were successfully evacuated from Anzac Cove and Sulva Bay. Another 35,000 men were evacuated from Helles in late December and early January 1917.

Ironically, the successful evacuation, in extreme weather conditions, under the nose of the enemy was easily the most successful element of the entire campaign.

The cost of this campaign was huge. Out of 480,000 Allied troops that took part in the campaign, 252,000 were casualties with 48,000 dead. On the other side it is estimated the Turks took 250,000 casualties.

Hand in Hand and Toe to Toe: The Battle of Loos

Let's be honest, the first half of 1915 had not gone well for the Allies. Champagne, Nueve Chapelle, Hill 60, Ypres and Gallipoli had all been disastrous and both Britain and France were struggling to conjure up a breakthrough.

This was the joyful backdrop for the preparation of what was to be the largest offensive of the year. The plan was that the British and French would advance hand-in-hand along a 20 mile front from Arras to La Bassée. The British would occupy the part of the line between Grenay and the La Bassée canal, with the French lining up from Champagne to Vimy. Their objectives were practically the same as last time, capture the intricate rail networks behind the German lines, and inflict as much damage on the German war machine as possible in the process.

Haig was decidedly uneasy. He didn't like the terrain he was being asked to advance over, he was in the middle of an acute shortage of guns and shells, and was at the limit of trained and equipped men in the field. He tried in vain to pull out but overwhelming political pressures meant he had no choice but to comply with his French friends.

But Haig did have one trick up his sleeve. Gas. Chlorine to be precise. And lots of it. The thick end of 5,000 cylinders of the stuff were carried to the front in preparation for the attack. It was time to give the enemy a dose of his own medicine. As well as being the first time the British had used gas in the war, this battle would also be noted as the first time the men from Kitchener's New Armies would see fighting on the Western Front.

Zero hour was set for 6.30am on the 25th September. Preparations at the front were far from secretive and as such the enemy knew something big was about to kick off. They sat in their trenches waiting for the bombardment, once that started they knew the attack would be imminent.

That bombardment started on 21st September and continued smashing the German lines until zero hour where it would lift to smash the German second line as per a meticulously prepared timetable. 250,000 shells were fired in those four days. Although the wind was far from perfect for a gas attack, Haig gave the go ahead for release at 5.50am on 25th September. Unfortunately, the release of the gas didn't go quite according to plan. In many places along the front the wind was so light it took over forty-five minutes to get anywhere near the German lines, in other places the gas actually blew back into the British lines. This catastrophe resulted in 2,632 British gas casualties and resulted in the British Tommy losing a lot of respect for his superior officers.

The results of the advance were also decidedly mixed. In some areas the bombardment had failed to smash the enemy wire and positions, in these areas German machine gunners had the time of their lives. The flat terrain offered nowhere for the attacking infantry to hide and many regiments were completely decimated. In these situations the attack quickly stalled, with many British soldiers forced back to their own lines.

Despite all of this, the right hand section of the front saw initial success, capturing the town of Loos. However, when they tried to continue the advance they were pinned down by machine-gun fire on the crest of Hill 70. Despite calling for artillery support at 10.30am none arrived until the late afternoon. By then it was too late. Reserves were also late coming up to help consolidate the gains. The reserves had been kept way behind the lines, and had to march for hours through crowded trenches and congested roads to get to the front. Once they got into the vicinity of Hill 70, they were taken apart by machine guns. This was the baptism of fire for Kitchener's New Armies. Other reserves didn't make it to the front until the early hours of the morning. Once again an opportunity to consolidate and build upon initial good progress had been lost.

This delay in reinforcements was crucial. The Germans managed to significantly add to their defensive structure overnight. The following day the British attacked again but advancing without any cover, they were annihilated by rifle, artillery and machine gun fire.

By nightfall on the 27th the attacking troops were practically spent. Hill 70 and other strategic positions had not been won and most were back to where they had started on the 25th. Once again the advance had broken into the enemy positions, but had failed to go beyond.

Sporadic fighting continued until 13th October, but the situation did not change. More than 61,000 casualties were sustained in the Battle of Loos. Kitchener's New Army units, rushed into the line after being in France a matter of days, suffered terribly – but they had proven they had what it takes to be a soldier on the Western Front. They had mixed it with enemy toe-to-toe, they may not have won this round, but they would be ready to come out swinging when the bell rang again.

Not Quite Trafalgar: The Battle of Jutland

Kaiser Wilhelm II had an obsession with the Royal Navy. Not a school boy obsession where he dreamt of sailing the world's seas, keeping them safe from pirates, belligerents and war mongers. No. He was instead obsessed with destroying it. Obsessed with building up his own fleet, the German High Seas Fleet, to be a match and even dominate the Royal Navy. In short he wanted the biggest, baddest navy of them all. It was an obsession that, even before the outbreak of war, had got up the noses of the Royal Navy. How dare Germany even attempt to build a navy that came anywhere near the British Grand Fleet. It was simply not cricket, and naval tempers had risen way before the opening bell of summer 1914.

By 1916, both fleets were straining at the leash and ready to go, like two heavyweight boxers at the pre-fight head-to-head. In the tale of the tape, they were well matched. Yes the British had a few more ships and bigger main guns, but the Germans had better armour protection and their secondary guns were much more effective at countering Destroyers.

The absence of aircraft at sea meant that figuring out the whereabouts of the enemy was down to decoding enemy messages, vigilant lookouts, and a bit of guesswork. On 31st May 1916 neither side really knew where each other was until scouting cruisers from both sides made contact as they both investigated a stationary Danish merchant ship. All of a sudden it was seconds out, round one.

The first round started when Admiral Beatty, commanding the British battle cruisers engaged with his counterpart, Admiral Hipper. Beatty thought he had the beating of Hipper and chased what he thought were retreating ships, to the south. During the chase each set of battle cruisers exchanged broadsides as they travelled along parallel courses. The British suffered badly. HMS Indefatigable blew up at 16.05 and was quickly followed by HMS Queen Mary at 16.25. HMS Lion, HMS Tiger and HMS Princess Royal were badly damaged. Round one to the Germans.

As the battle moved south the Germans came into range of the big British Battleships who started scoring hits from a distance of ten miles. Nice work. Round two to the British.

However, just a few minutes later Beatty got word that he was heading straight towards the entire German Fleet, and they were in range. Bugger. He immediately ordered his ships to turn around and head north towards Admiral Jellicoe and the remainder of the British Grand Fleet. With a bit of luck he would lead the Germans nicely into a trap. Round three was perhaps a draw.

The Germans did give chase, and indeed they got a nasty surprise when they fell under a huge bombardment from Jellicoe's battle fleet, which they thought had been too far north to be of any consequence. At 18.30 Admiral Scheer found himself surrounded to the north and north-west. The only option was to turn east. The Grand Fleet threw everything they had at Scheer, who ordered an about turn to every ship in his command at 18.35. Executed perfectly, within a few minutes the German High Seas Fleet slipped into the murk and out of sight. The British were sure they had sunk a number of ships, but in reality only one was lost. Whereas the British had lost HMS Warrior and HMS Invincible, and HMS Warspite was severely damaged. The Germans were ahead on points going into round five.

As the Germans fled, Jellicoe refused to follow directly, fearful of a minefield or submarine trap. Instead he turned southeast, then south in an effort to cut Scheer off indirectly.

Then, inexplicably, Scheer turned his fleet to the North, and basically steamed straight back into the heart of the Grand Fleet. Jellicoe thought Christmas had come early and at 19.10 he let the Germans have it in a big way. Within twenty minutes, one German destroyer was sunk and many had taken an absolute pounding before the German fleet were able to about turn and retreat. This time Jellico went on the chase, heading southwest in an effort to intercept. And intercept he did, sighting the enemy at 20.15 just before sunset. The guns flashed in the gathering gloom and more German ships were destroyed and damaged. At 20.30 Scheer sent six of his ships forward to occupy the British guns while he gathered the rest of his fleet and fled to the West.

The Battle of Jutland was over. It would turn out to be the largest and the last of the great battleship battles. Never again would either side meet each other in such numbers. In the immediate aftermath of the battle the British public were upset, they had expected another Trafalgar. On the other hand the Germans celebrated Jutland as a victory, and yes they did inflict more losses on the British than the other way around. However, the Grand Fleet was straight back in training and was ready to fight again by the 2nd June, whereas the German High Fleet was crippled for months. It never really recovered and was never risked again in a North Sea battle.

Despite not delivering 'another Trafalgar', The Royal Navy had retained dominance of the seas.

Ils Ne Passeront Pas! The Battle of Verdun

As dawn broke on 1916, Germany was in a tricky position. Those pesky Russians in the east didn't know when they were beaten and on the Western Front it was clear that their initial plan of taking Paris quickly was beyond them. In the short term at least they needed another way to defeat France. They had to draw the French into an artillery slug-fest. A huge all-out fight that would consume all of the French resources and manpower until they had nothing left. For this plan to work they would need a target that the French would defend until the last man, regardless of losses.

That place was Verdun, a fortress city with a special place in French hearts. It had been an important fortress town since the Romans; in the Franco-Prussian war of 1870-71 it was the last fortress to fall and in the following decade it was bolstered and reinforced to withstand any future attacks. The town of Verdun meant a great deal to the French public, emotionally more than strategically, and they would defend it until the last man if necessary. This was what Eric von Falkenhayn, the German Chief of Staff, counted on when putting his master plan together.

The brutal plan was this: The German Army had to kill more Frenchmen than the French could kill Germans. It really was that crude. No territorial gains were required; it was simply, as Falkenhayn had suggested, to 'bleed France white'.

Verdun was a perfect choice for the attack; German communications around the city were much better than the defenders, who had to rely on only one road and one narrow gauge railway, both of which were in range of the German guns.

The city was only very lightly defended as the big guns from the mighty forts had been removed for use elsewhere on the front. Verdun was basically there for the taking.

The German artillery opened up on 21st February 1916. Across a six mile front, 1,220 guns chucked over a million shells onto Verdun and the surrounding area over a hellish nine hours period. That's a lot of shells by the way. Not surprisingly, such a fire storm annihilated almost everything in its path. Barbed wire was shredded, trees were shattered, trenches were demolished, and men were destroyed. At 4pm that day, the guns lifted and the assaulting infantry advanced. Those French soldiers who had somehow survived the bombardment fought heroically, they defended to the death, inch by inch, but gradually the overwhelming attacking force took its toll, and the Germans advanced on, albeit slowly.

In one area, soldiers led by Colonel Emile (who had been warning his superiors of the risk of attack at Verdun for months) numbered 1,200 on the morning of the 21st. By nightfall they were just 300; the woods they were defending were reduced to matchwood.

The cost on this first day for France was huge, over 10,000 casualties, but the herculean defence of Verdun had slowed up the attackers and once again the critical timing of Falkenhayn's plan was thrown off course. In some places only advances of 500 metres or so had been achieved, instead of the seven or eight miles that were planned. Despite this, the Germans methodically smashed seven bells out of Verdun over the next couple of days. Eventually, on 24th February, they broke through the French first line. The second line fell soon afterwards, and the third line was not even built yet. The Germans were five miles from Verdun, and not much stood in their way.

By rights, Verdun should have fallen to the Germans that night. But for some reason the attackers suddenly became very cautious and advanced very slowly. Maybe they were expecting lots of reserves to suddenly appear from a bush, or maybe the plan actually wasn't to take Verdun at all, (remember the overall strategy wasn't territory gain, but the death of the French army). Whatever the reason, they missed the golden opportunity that night.

Joffre was understandably nervous. On the 26th he put General Pétain in charge of the army at Verdun. Pétain immediately re-organised the line and orchestrated a more robust artillery response. He also made sure the supply routes to the front were kept open at all times, this made a huge difference as new men, weapons and equipment finally arrived at the front. By the 28th the German offensive had started to bog down, and with the much improved artillery situation, the French were actually starting to give it back to the Germans.

In an effort to eliminate French artillery, the Germans launched another monumental artillery barrage and offensive on 6th March. They wanted to take control of two ridges, Côte 304 and the beautifully named Morte Homme (Dead Man's) ridge. Ground was gained but Morte Homme was not in German hands until 29th May, and not before some savage bloodletting.

A few weeks later saw another monster offensive from the Germans. This time they even threw Phosgene gas at the French. The Germans gained ground and pushed the French back once again, capturing the town of Fleury on 23rd June. At this time General Robert Nivelle, recently promoted to the command of the French Second Army, issued an Order of the Day which ended with the infamous rallying cry: Ils ne passeront pas! (They shall not pass!).

Fighting continued throughout the summer and autumn, but with the British diversionary attack on the Somme taking up valuable German resources, combined with new tactics instigated by Nivelle, such as concentrated counter-attacks using a creeping barrage (a safety curtain of shell fire that the advancing infantry could 'hide' behind as they advanced), the tables were slowly turning. Indeed, it was the French that started to advance with a series of successful counter-attacks throughout October and November. Fleury was back in French hands by 24th October. By mid-December the Germans had been pushed back far enough to render Verdun safe.

The battle of Verdun was a tear up of epic proportions. The French estimate losses at around 550,000 men, with the Germans estimated at over 450,000. About half of all casualties were killed.

Britain's Blackest Day: The Somme Offensive 1916

The Somme offensive was the main Allied attack along the Western Front in 1916. Launched on 1st July along a nineteen mile front line north of the River Somme between Amiens and Péronne, it eventually ended on 18th November due to bad weather.

Originally intended to be an offensive dominated by French forces, with the British in support, its primary objective would be to smash the German army and deplete their manpower reserves. This was never going to be a nimble, clever campaign. Oh no; just brute strength and attrition please waiter.

As it was their show, the decision to launch the offensive in the Somme region was down to the French High Command. The decision was taken based upon the location of available manpower and resource rather than any grand strategy or plan. Haig preferred an attack in the north of Belgium to check the growing U-boat problem emanating from the Belgian ports but the politics of the situation forced him yet again to follow the French lead. So everything was agreed. Hands were shook, backs were patted and cigars lit. The 'big push' was pencilled in for August 1916.

But, the Germans messed up all the plans when they launched their own offensive at Verdun at the beginning of 1916. Suddenly the French were the ones being 'bled white' and within a few months it was clear that France would not be in any fit state to lead a major offensive. In fact it was touch and go as to whether they would survive as a fighting unit. They needed help from Britain to divert German manpower and resource away from Verdun, and they needed it fast.

As a result the date of the attack was brought forward to the beginning of July, and it was now a large scale British diversionary attack, with only minimal French support. Planning passed to Haig, who sat at his desk and slowly stroked his moustache as he devised his master plan. It was game on.

The plan was simple: Mass more guns than have ever been massed before to fire more shells than had ever been fired before, for longer than had ever been done before. This would completely smash the German defences, cut their wire to smithereens and shatter the resolve and morale of the enemy soldiers. Then, the infantry, some 750,000 men (of which a large portion were made up from Kitchener's new Pals Battalions), would advance and consolidate the positions, with cavalry at the ready in order to attempt a complete breakthrough if the opportunity arose. Simple.

Despite a monster eight-day bombardment, a mixture of poor quality ammunition and world-class underground German bunkers resulted in failure. Wire was not cut, morale had not been broken, defences were still intact and when the infantry attacked the German positions at 7.30am on 1st July the German machine gunners and artillery were ready and waiting.

The result was nothing short of a bloodbath. The British Army suffered almost 58,000 casualties on this one day. A third of these were killed. To this day it stands out as the blackest moment in the Army's illustrious history. Apart from the odd isolated success the large bulk of the British infantry were either cut down in No

Man's Land or forced back to their own lines. Ironically it was the French that made the best progress towards the south of the front.

Despite everything, Haig persisted with the offensive in the following days. Advances were made, but these were limited and mostly repulsed. On the 11th July the first line of German trenches were secured. On that day German troops were transferred from Verdun to contribute to the German defence, doubling the number of men available for the defence.

Like punch-drunk cage fighters, both sides thought they were one decisive blow away from total victory, so they kept smashing each other in the face, time and again. There were minor successes such as the Australian capture of Pozieres on the 23rd July, but these were isolated victories and could not be capitalised upon.

On the 15th September, the British attacked again in the Battle of Flers-Courcelette. It was here that the tank made its operational debut, and although it scared the hell out of the enemy, these early 'land ships' failed to make a great impact due to reliability issues and a lack of tactical expertise on how to best utilise these new weapons, and the advance only gained a mile or two.

The sparring carried on until the November snow forced the final suspension of operations. Allied forces had gained a slither of tortured landscape eight miles across at its deepest point.

Over a million men became casualties during this bitter struggle, with Britain and her Empire suffering to the tune of 419,654 men, wounded and killed. However, the Germans suffered terribly too (around 500,000 casualties), and they were forced to stop attacking Verdun allowing the French army to dust itself down and regroup. So while the tactics of Haig remain controversial even to this day, the offensive achieved the desired effect: relieve the pressure on the French at Verdun, and inflict huge casualties on the Germans. So from a purely military point of view, he could be excused for saying 'job done'.

France Look to Russia: The Brusilov Offensive

While the French were taking a beating at Verdun, they pleaded to the Allies to launch their own offensives to draw German troops away from that particular part of France. While the British planned their attack on the Somme, the Russians were weighing up their options in the east. On 15th May, the Austrians launched a significant attack on the Trentio region and threatened to overwhelm the Italian Army, the Russians were again asked to intervene and help draw attacking troops away – this time Austrian resources. To be honest, the cautious Russian military leadership were not keen; they didn't think they had enough guns and shells to back up such a large attack in the south. They were planning their own push in the north and didn't really fancy taking resources and material from that plan to use in the south.

Enter Alexia Brusilov, a Russian general who thought he could not only put together an effective offensive that would knock Austria out of the Italian front, but do it without any new reinforcements and only minimal extra equipment. Almost all the other Russian generals were surprised, many were sceptical, but Brusilov had a plan, the Tsar liked what he heard and the offensive was approved.

It was time to get busy.

Brusilov was a clever chap. He had figured out the greatest dichotomy of the war so far. The generally accepted offensive strategy of attacking with large numbers on a narrow front with a huge preliminary bombardment was flawed for three main reasons: Firstly, all elements of surprise were completely thrown out of the window; as soon as any side started lobbing large amounts of shells in any particular sector for a prolonged period of time, the other side pretty much knew that something heavy was about to kick off and they could make the necessary arrangements. Also, the huge amount of men and material needed for such large offensives made it very difficult to conceal from the enemy, especially if their air force was active, it would be very easy for pilots to spot long streams of men and equipment being brought up to the front line in preparation for the attack. Secondly, by attacking on a narrow front, it allowed for defensive re-enforcements from other areas of the front to be positioned to the relatively small affected area. Thirdly, if and when the breakthrough occurred, it was very difficult to keep the momentum going, as guns and reserves were often slow to move forwards and continue the attack.

In order to negate as many of these issues as possible, Brusilov had a plan. He knew it was vital to disrupt the enemy's reserves, so that when the breakthrough came the attacking forces did not run straight into a large counter-attack from fresh enemy troops. This, in his plan, would be achieved by surprise. Guns were to be concealed, troops and supplies were hidden in underground bunkers, if any overt preparations were needed, they were to be carried out up and down the entire line so as to give no clue as to the location of any attack. Also, the offensive would not be limited to a single attack on a small narrow front; there would be many attacks up and down the line, each with a significant breadth of front. Reserves were to be brought up right to the front, so they could take advantage of any breakthrough. Artillery officers would also be part of the front line troops, directing fire right from the front line.

Preparation was meticulous and methodical; something often missing on the Eastern Front, Brusilov's men were going to attack a very well defended line. Mines, some electric fences, barbed wire, and well-dug trenches had all been built by the Austro-Hungarian forces there. However, Brusilov had produced very detailed maps and he had ordered his officers to study these maps in great detail. His advance trenches - dug for his men for the start of the campaign - were less than 100 metres from the Austro-Hungarian front lines. Brusilov would have four separate armies attacking the Austrians. Almost 600,000 Russian troops were ready and had taken their seats for the 'big show'. The curtains were due to be raised on 4th June.

When the guns opened up on 4th June, in the northern sector of the line, it was short, sharp, and very accurate. Much of the first defensive line of the Austrians was smashed to pieces and the attacking Russians had little trouble overrunning the initial lines. As they drove deeper into enemy territory, shock troops went out in-front, seeking out the weak points of the line and breaching deep into the defensive structure, cutting communication lines and generally causing havoc – allowing the following reserves to come in numbers and consolidate the gains. The Austrians in the north were being routed and the alarm was quickly sounded to HQ – reinforcements were needed and needed quick.

But, in the south, there was another crisis for the Austrians. The Russians had also attacked on the Romanian border and were causing all kinds of trouble down there. The Austrian army was on the retreat – but where to send the reserves? Reserves could not be placed effectively and as a result the entire army was being pushed backwards. It was chaos.

In the centre, the Russian advances were less spectacular, and one of the armies, led by General Evert failed to get going at all.

Notwithstanding the small setback in the centre of the front, to the north and to the south, the Russians pushed forward with wild enthusiasm. They had quickly advanced over sixty miles taking 350,000 prisoners en route. In emergency meetings the German Chief-of-Staff, von Falkenhayn persuaded the Austrians to retreat and fall back to a more stable line close to good railway links. This enabled troops from other areas, including the German troops from the Western Front to be pushed into the breach.

Meanwhile, the Russian advance was slowing down. The troops were exhausted and had stretched supply lines to breaking point. They had run out of ammunition and water and had little or no communications with each other. As a result, Brusilov's forces advanced on two lines within their sector that went in the opposite direction to the other, thus diminishing their effectiveness. The attack in the centre never really materialised, and the troops were sent to the southern sector. This was exactly what Brusilov didn't want as now the enemy would be able to track the movement of troops and know where the next attack was coming from. Sure enough, the next attack in the south ran straight into a nest of highly trained and experienced German troops and was repulsed.

The spectacular gains of the first weeks had dried up and by mid-August the attack had pretty much spluttered to a halt.

With over a million casualties on either side, this was one of the deadliest battles of the war, and there was no real breakthrough to speak of. However, the Austro – Hungarian army was practically destroyed, they would not be able to launch another meaningful attack again.

Fromelles: The Worst 24 Hours in Australia's Entire History

An attack in and around the villages of Fleurbaix and Fromelles was initially pencilled in as part of a widening of the Somme offensive. However, successes on the Somme were not forthcoming and the relevance of an attack around Fromelles was largely dismissed by the middle of July. However, Lieutenant-General Sir Richard Haking (GOC XI Corps), the local commander of the area was still keen to press ahead with the operation, despite no clear objective or plan.

The rough idea, hastily modified from the original plan, was to stop the Germans moving troops from this sector further south to re-enforce the Somme area. This attack would also be the first to involve the Australians on the Western Front. Their 5th Division had landed in France just days before, and would be thrown in right at the deep end. Assisted by the British 61st Division.

The attack would centre around a salient – nicknamed 'Sugar Loaf' due to its size and shape. Sugar Loaf was relatively small but commanded all the high ground in the area and had unrestricted views on all sides. Sugar Loaf was held by the 6th Bavarian Reserve Division, and they had built a very solid and intricate defensive position. Taking the Loaf would not be easy, and would need some clever tactics, perhaps a surprise attack under darkness using a small number of elite troops.

After careful consideration, the clever chaps of the Army High Command decided that a huge artillery bombardment, followed by a full frontal mass infantry attack in broad daylight, would be the best way to go. The artillery bombardment would definitely smash the defenders to little pieces, and the infantry would be able to amble up the hill, cigars on the go, and take the positions.

Sound familiar? Unfortunately it seems that the lessons of The Somme were not being fully heeded.

For seven or so hours before zero, the German lines were shelled to bits. The problem was, the maps that the British Officers had that showed the position of the German lines were out of date. The Germans had actually pulled back a few hundred yards to a new defensive line. Those shells, all 200,000 of them, fell on empty earth and reduced the landscape to a muddy bog, devoid of cover – which, in the end would prove disastrous for the attacking infantry.

After the bombardment the Australian and British troops advanced. Some elements of the Australian contingent actually made it to their first objective; however there were no Germans there, just mud and more mud. From their new positions the Germans made easy work of the attackers. With no cover, they didn't stand a chance.

The British and Australian troops who advanced on the right flank of the attack didn't even have the chance to reach their objective – they were literally cut to pieces by machine guns as they crossed No Man's Land.

Later in the evening, the British asked the Australian 15th Brigade to join up with a renewed assault on the German lines at 9pm. However, this attack was cancelled, but, incredibly, someone forgot to tell the Australians, who advanced again, alone, and suffered terribly.

During a German counter attack the Australian forces were split into two, each side becoming increasingly isolated and vulnerable to complete encirclement. The order to retreat at daybreak was given, however by the time the retreat had begun; those Germans had set up even more machine gun posts and inflicted devastating casualties on the retreating Australian troops.

It was not a good introduction to battle for the Australians. After a little over twenty-four hours of fighting, they had suffered 5,533 casualties (killed, wounded or prisoners). The British had fared slightly better, but still, 1,547 casualties were not insignificant. Not one inch of ground had been won. It was a complete disaster.

The Australian War Memorial describes the battle as "the worst 24 hours in Australia's entire history."

Metal Monsters: Tanks

In among the Flanders fields of autumn 1914 the landscape hadn't yet succumbed to the merciless pounding of the guns, and farmers still harvested their crops and went about their normal business. It was, among other things, the sight of some of this agricultural machinery that got a few of the clever chaps from the BEF thinking. Wouldn't it be a great idea if they could have an armoured, motorised gun to support the infantry when things got a bit frantic in the field? It would be even better if the aforementioned armoured mobile gun could be loaded onto caterpillar tracks like some farm equipment, meaning easier movement across a wider variety of terrain.

A formal memorandum on 'special devices' was compiled in December 1914 in which such equipment was officially mentioned for the first time. Simultaneously the Royal Navy were working on similar ideas. The naval minister, a certain Winston Churchill, having read the army report as well as being involved in the Navy ideas, put together a Technical Landship Committee (taken from the Navy's code-name for some of their ideas) in February 1915.

In June that year the committee had formulated their technical want list. They demanded a land speed of 4mph, 'rapid' all round manoeuvrability, a range of twelve miles, and some big guns, all bolted to a caterpillar track. On the basis of seeing a wooden mock up in September, Sir Douglas Haig, Commander-in-Chief of the BEF, was impressed enough to order forty and went off dreaming of these new machines ripping through the German defences with ease, scattering the enemy and destroying their positions. Prime Minster Lloyd George approved the project and production started in April 1916.

Imaginatively named after their coded transportation name of 'water tanks' the first batch of Mk 1 tanks entered service with the Heavy Section of the Machine Gun Corp, later to become the Tank Corps, in June 1916. British High Command thought the war was as good as won.

The day when the tank was to make its operational debut was pencilled in to be the 15th September, 1916. Tactics and strategy were mulled over for months and months. In the end, Haig, going against the advice of his field officers, decided to mass all 49 serviceable tanks in an attack on a limited objective during the Battle of Flers-Courcelette. The press had a field day with wild reports of masses of Germans soldiers running for their lives at the sight of these metal monsters, of them being squashed by the huge metal tracks (remember the top speed of these beauties) and general mass hysteria in the enemy ranks as the gallant and noble British Tommy, rode atop his iron horse tearing an unstoppable march towards the German lines. Towards victory, and to freedom.

Reality, however, was a little different, and although the sight of the tanks did cause a good deal of confusion in the German lines, only a fraction of the tanks were able to advance any meaningful distance. The fact is there were a few... er, issues. Firstly the crews were not properly trained. Then there is the fact that the tanks themselves were not properly tested as they were rushed into the field. As a consequence, they were mechanically very unreliable in the field, with many breaking down before they got anywhere near the enemy lines. They had practically zero visibility; the crew had to rely on messages tapped on the hull of the tanks by the infantrymen. Then there were the conditions inside. If the crew were not poisoned by the engine fumes, then they were slowly boiled by the insane heat inside the cabin. If they survived that lot, then there was always the possibility of being burnt to a crisp in a fire ball after either being hit by the enemy or just because of a random act of sudden incineration.

Despite all this, the British High Command loved them and ordered more, and to be fair to the manufacturers, the subsequent new versions were much improved. In November 1917 at Cambrai, a massed attack over firm ground proved a stunning success, only spoilt on the second day of the advance by the failure to exploit the initial gains on the first day of the battle. It is this result that seemingly sealed the (positive) fate for the tank in future British offensives.

However, during WW1 at least, partly due to design weaknesses and reliability issues, and partly due to poor tactics, the tank was reduced to being only a bit part player in the Allied victory. Their subsequent reputation as the fire breathing monster that dashed the enemy, evident perhaps more in Britain than anywhere else was largely created by post-war writers and commentary, often with their own agenda.

Another Verdun: The Second Battle of The Aisne

Let's not mess around; the Allies took an absolute beating in 1916. Verdun, The Somme and Fromelles were all unmitigated, murderous disasters that were simply not sustainable. Something had to change otherwise the Allies would rapidly find themselves staring down the barrel of defeat. On the other side of the wire, the Germans were fairing no better; they too had endured enormous losses of men and resources, especially at Verdun and on the Somme. So, with the memory of 1916 still painfully fresh, both sides saw the beginning of 1917 as an opportunity to pause for thought, take stock of the situation and make new plans for the coming year.

For the French, they had put General Robert Nivelle in charge of things after his good work at Verdun. He planned an offensive in the Aisne/Arras area of the front. It was practically the same plan as the French assault in the same sector in 1915. Only this time there were more guns and a couple of tanks thrown in for good measure. The British would help by attacking Arras, while the French would have a go in the Aisne sector.

The Germans were also thinking about their 1917 strategy. They were suffering too and in dire need of improved efficiency all along the line. There was no strategic rhyme or reason for the position of the current trench lines which dated mostly from 1914. So, they pulled back to the strongly fortified Hindenburg Line (which they had been building since the winter of 1916) in February and March 1917. This new line shortened their front by over 30 miles which released thousands of troops from front line duty and made defence, organisation and transportation along the lines much easier.

This ruined Nivelle's plans. He had put in a lot of work into this offensive based on the precise locations of the enemy guns. Now they had all moved, he had to do everything again. He persevered however; with a few alterations the offensive would still go ahead. He was very aware that France was still convalescing after the terror of 1916, and he publically promised that this new battle would deliver the good news his country badly needed. He also promised that if there was no apparent breakthrough after two days of fighting, he would call the whole thing off. He did not want another Verdun.

Trouble was, in the build up to the attack Nivelle did a lot of talking; to his staff, to journalists, to friends, to anyone who would listen. Not surprisingly when the attack did come, the enemy were ready and waiting.

The French guns opened up on 2nd April. Never before had there been so many French guns firing so many French shells. By 5th May over 5,000 artillery pieces had fired eleven million shells into the German defences. Surely the enemy couldn't survive that kind of a hammering? The thing was, yet again, the artillery bombardment failed to smash the defences. The Hindenburg Line was a masterpiece in defensive design, and the reserves, all seventeen Divisions of them (approx. 255,000 men, plus all their kit, guns, horses and supplies), were physically out of reach of artillery range. When the infantry advanced on 16th April, it was like lambs to the slaughter.

The Germans occupied heavily fortified high ground and inflicted massive losses on the French attackers; approximately 40,000 casualties were inflicted in the first day alone as well as destroying 150 or so tanks. Another large offensive on the 17th east of Rheims fared no better. On each day Nivelle's main technical innovation, the creeping barrage, failed miserably, continually falling short and firing on their own men.

Despite his earlier promises, Nivelle continued to press on with more offensives with predictable results. By 20th April, despite some isolated gains it had become obvious that all efforts had failed. In five days they had lost as many men as in one month at Verdun. It was becoming all too familiar for the soldiers in the front line, and discontent started to run rife with many soldiers refusing to carry out orders to advance further.

Over the coming weeks the offensive was scaled back, although it was in this period when they secured their biggest accomplishment; the capture of a three mile stretch of the Chemin des Dames Ridge (part of the Hindenburg Line). Despite this the battle drew to a close on 9th May as the newly appointed French Chief, General Henri Pétain, turned his attention to restoring the morale of his wrecked army.

If this battle had been fought in early 1915 it may have been viewed as a partial success, however with another 130,000 French names placed on the ever growing casualty list it was viewed as yet another futile waste of life.

Another Verdun.

Defence in Depth: Arras & Vimy Ridge

Part of Nivelle's grand plan of 1917 was to use the British and Canadian forces in a diversionary attack at Arras, just to the north of the main French offensive on the Aisne.

As they had done further south, the Germans had also retreated towards the Hindenburg Line in the Arras area causing the British the same planning problems that had hindered the French. Wherever possible the enemy had positioned themselves on the reverse slopes of hills and had adopted a 'defence in depth' strategy. This amounted to leaving the front lines relatively empty apart from a number of machine gun nests designed to inflict as much damage onto the attacking troops as possible. These men would then retreat, pulling the attacking infantry along with them to such an extent that the attackers would advance beyond the protective shield of their artillery. Then they would be destroyed by huge counter attacks.

This 'defence in depth' technique utilised by the Hindenburg Line was very effective and caused carnage and devastation throughout the ranks of any attacking force. However, the world 'Line' is a bit of a misnomer. It wasn't anything like a continuous line, but a collection of heavily defended and fortified areas along the front. A perfect example of this was the Arras area. The region to the south of the village of Arras was heavily defended, but just a few miles north towards the Vimy Ridge it was a different story. German defences here were in range of the Allied guns; their trenches were on the forward slopes of hills and were heavily manned. An attack in this area could prove more fruitful.

The attack commenced on 9th April after a steady five day artillery bombardment that had given the Germans all the notice they needed to prepare for a fight. The attacking troops were split into two groups; the Canadians in the north were to capture the Vimy Ridge, with the British forces to the south, just in front of the village of Arras.

A notable part of this attack was the use of tunnels as a method of troop transportation. The village of Arras had a huge number of tunnels and sewers underneath it which the Royal Engineers widened and extended way out into No Man's Land. Troops could be amassed for the attack in almost complete secrecy.

This element of surprise was a major factor in the Canadian successes on the Vimy Ridge. Advancing in a snowstorm, surprise was so complete that enemy trenches were occupied before the machine gunners were able to get to their guns. The artillery also pulled off a perfect creeping barrage which destroyed the German first and second line defences and enabled the Canadians to advance two miles in one day. By the 12th they had captured the entire ridge. It was viewed as a spectacular success, but it was not without cost, with over 14,000 Canadians killed or wounded in this advance.

The British forces to the south of Vimy Ridge also exploited the tunnel network and creeping barrage to their advantage. In this area, as in the north, they faced more traditional German defences instead of the tougher 'defence in depth' fortifications. Even though the attack was expected they too quickly achieved their goals, moving through the initial lines of German defence taking thousands of prisoners on the way.

Whilst the advances in the north and the centre had enjoyed initial success, those attacks in the south of the sector had different luck. This sector received the smallest artillery support which largely failed to damage the German defences or cut the barbed wire. General Gough, in charge of this sector, wanted to delay the offensive in the light of this lack of artillery back up, but he was seduced by the success enjoyed elsewhere and wanted to be part of what he thought would be a great victory. Despite weak artillery and despite not having enough tanks, he gave the go ahead for the attack on the strongpoints of Bullecourt and Moncy-le-Preux. Due to technical delays concerning the tanks, the offensive didn't commence until 11th April. In this one small action the tanks got lost, the artillery didn't happen and the attacking Australian Division lost 2,258 out of 3,000 men without gaining any significant territory and inflicting only minimal damage onto the enemy. From that day on General Gough would never be able to step foot in Australia without fear of his life. Let's just say he was not well liked.

Elsewhere things started to slow down as the Germans managed to bring up large numbers of reserves to bolster its defence. Once more this battle proved that it was possible to break into and capture enemy lines, but to break through completely was a very different matter. By rights, the battle should have been called off by the 12th or 13th, but Britain was obliged to help out the French and continue the diversionary attack so the Germans couldn't switch their forces to the south. So, the fighting continued into May with some particularly vicious encounters around Bullecourt.

Despite the failure to breakthrough, the Arras offensive, particularly the North and Central areas, were deemed a success and Vimy Ridge was considered an important gain, both strategically and psychologically. But with a casualty list containing over 165,000 names, it didn't come cheap.

There's Mutiny in the Air: French Unrest

The Nivelle offensive had broken the French army. By the end of April 1917 they had suffered the thick end of one million dead; the infantry were, quite frankly, fed up, they just didn't want to do this anymore.

The mutiny was never a coherent, joined up movement, it was more a series of independent reactions to a combination of factors such as the huge casualties, the disappointment at the failure of yet another 'dead-cert' offensive, the grim conditions in the trenches, poor pay and limited rest time. All these issues had been simmering within the infantry for some time, it just needed a spark to light the fuse – the Nivelle offensive was that spark.

Now, the French rank and file were a civilised bunch, they didn't try to massacre the officer class, they didn't burn down villages or fight amongst themselves. They just refused to return to the front line trenches. Some soldiers disappeared into nearby villages, others, when ordered to return to the front by their officers, simply sat on the floor and refused to move.

New French Commander-in-Chief, General Phillipe Pétain, acted swiftly to quash the dissenters. He embarked on an extensive tour of the front, visiting ninety Divisions (the total size of the French army at the time was 113 Divisions), listening to the soldiers and discussing their issues and grievances in person. This was a rare example of the top man in the army listening and empathising with the ordinary man in the trenches. Not only did he listen, but he actually put processes together to make things better for the soldiers. After this tour he immediately introduced increased rations, better provisions for leave and rest as well as improved medical facilities. He also re-iterated the predicament their country was in; if the army gave up, then what would happen? They would be over-run by Germany and every Frenchman would be force fed bratwurst and made to wear Lederhosen. Not a pretty thought.

As a result, the French Army was back in position by the end of July. Although more than 23,000 soldiers were convicted of mutinous behaviour, harsh repression (executions, hard labour etc.) were kept to a minimum.

It has been suggested by eminent French historian Guy Pedroncini, that the mutinies affected forty-nine infantry divisions, this equates to 43% of the entire French Infantry. As a consequence, much of the French held sectors on the Western Front were dangerously weak, however credit must be given to the French authorities here as they kept news of the mutinies almost completely secret, thus the integrity of the line was not compromised.

The army was pronounced fit for action once more in August 1917, but in reality it was in a very delicate state. The French leaders knew this and restricted actions to only small operations, more for show than anything else.

Revolution: The Collapse of the Eastern Front

Mutiny was not just confined to France. 1917 had been an 'interesting' year for Russia too. In February, food riots, demonstrations, and a mutiny at the Petrograd Garrison forced Tsar Nicholas II to abdicate as war still continued. Despite widespread unrest and anti-war feelings that were rapidly spreading, not just though the civilian population, but filtering also through to the trenches at the front, Paul Miliukov, Russia's new Foreign Minister, declared on 17th March that Russia would remain loyal to her Allies and continue the fight. There would be no Russian exit from the war.

However, the condition and morale of the Russian army was on a steep downward slide. More and more orders were ignored, soldiers went AWOL, or simply refused to move up to forward facing positions. By late autumn, the situation was desperate.

On 3rd November 1917 Russian troops on the Baltic Front had thrown down their weapons and refused to fight. The next day the Petrograd garrison, holding over 150,000 soldiers, was ordered to go to the Front, but were urged to stay by the Bolsheviks. Whilst the leaders of the garrison tried to decide what to do, the Provisional Government ordered troops outside the city to enter Petrograd and take control. They refused.

By the evening of 6th November the Bolsheviks had taken control of many of the vital buildings of the city including railway stations, the bank and the telephone office. By 7th November, the Winter Palace, which housed the Government was surrounded by almost 15,000 soldiers and sailors committed to revolution. They were backed up by a couple of naval destroyers and the cruiser Aurora, which fired a few blanks at the palace to show that the Revolutionaries were not messing about.

In the early hours of 8th November, the Bolsheviks had overrun the Palace and taken control. Vladimir Illych Lenin, head of the Bolsheviks, was now the ruler of the Russian capital. One of the first things he did was to issue the 'Decree of Peace' calling for an end to all hostilities.

As a war making power, Russia was finished.

On November 19th Leon Trotsky, in charge of foreign policy for the Bolsheviks, called for an armistice on all fronts. Not surprisingly this request fell on deaf ears. So, the Russian put together plans for a separate peace with the Central Powers, and on 1st December a Bolshevik armistice party left Petrograd bound for the Eastern Front. They crossed into the German lines the following day and were transported by train to the former Russian fortress of Brest-Litovsk. There they began negotiations with Germans, Austrians, Bulgarians and Turks to return the entire Eastern Front to a state of peace.

On 15th December the negotiators at Brest-Litovsk declared the official end of all fighting on the Eastern Front. For Germany this meant the end of the two-front war that had been such a huge burden to them since 1914.

After the ink was dry, Russia was effectively relieved of almost 25% of her entire population, vast tracts of land and a huge proportion of her coal mining capability. From a territory point of view, most of the land that was ceded was non-Russian speaking areas which had been absorbed through military activities over the last few hundred years, such as modern day Finland, Estonia, Latvia, Lithuania and Ukraine.

With the eastern front as good as dead, the Central Powers could now concentrate all their effort in the west. The transfer of troops, guns and equipment began in earnest.

Room For One More? America Joins in

Truth be told, America was very reluctant to enter the war, and you can understand why. It was fought thousands of miles away, between a bunch of mad Europeans that all spoke funny and ate too much cheese and sausage. Add to this the hugely diverse make up of America (there were over ten million Americans that were either first or second generation German at the time of war), not to mention the Canadian/French relationship, and the large Italian, Irish, Polish and other Slav populations all over the country. Taking sides here would be divisive both in Europe and at home. It just wasn't worth the hassle.

Keeping neutral was also good for business. Exports to Western Europe more than trebled from 1914 to 1916 as the warring nations concentrated all their manufacturing efforts on making guns and bullets. Then there was the increase in trade to other parts of the world due to lower competition from Europe. The coffers were full and no Americans were getting shot, it was a win-win situation.

Germany pushed American patience in 1915 with the sinking of RMS Lusitania by a submarine (U-20) off the coast of Ireland. Lusitania was a cruise liner and sank with 1,198 casualties, 124 of whom were US nationals. Despite public outrage in America, nothing more than a stern letter condemning the action was sent to Berlin. It was tantamount to putting Germany on the naughty step.

Fast forward to 1917 and Berlin decided it would be fun to commence unrestricted submarine warfare. Basically, any ship would be fair game. They knew that this might upset the Americans and bring them closer to entering the war, so to pre-empt this Germany sought to buy the support of Mexico. The German foreign minister, Dr Alfred von Zimmerman sent a message to his Mexican counterpart suggesting an active alliance with Germany would, among other things, enable Mexico to reclaim the territories they lost to America some seventy years previous; those of Texas, Arizona and New Mexico. They also suggested that Japan was also interested in holding hands and making friends. Unfortunately for Zimmerman, this, and other messages, were intercepted by the Royal Navy and shown to President Thomas Woodrow Wilson on 24th February. Because of this note (which was put in the press a few days later), the unrestricted submarine war and a general mistrust of Mexicans, popular American sentiment swung wildly towards a war with Germany.

Pressure was also applied to Wilson to declare war from the bankers and financial community. Over the course of the war America had lent the Allies (particularly France and UK) a fair few dollars to keep the guns oiled and the bayonets sharp. By 1917 France and UK had together racked up an impressive $2.25billion in loans. In contrast, US loans to Germany amounted to $27million. The US bankers were nervous; Russia was close to revolution, the French army was in mutiny, Britain was exhausted; the picture wasn't pretty for the Allies in 1917, and America knew that if the Allies lost the war and couldn't pay back their loans the American banking system would be on its knees. They wanted Wilson to send over the boys to bail out the Allies so they could pay their bills.

On 21st March, the US tanker Healdton was torpedoed whilst sailing in specially declared 'safe waters' just off the Dutch coast with the loss of twenty crewmen. President Wilson ordered Congress to meet on 2nd April – it was here that he asked for permission to go to war. The vote for war was unanimous and America declared war on the Germany on 6th April.

It was official. America had dealt herself 'in'.

A Much Needed Boost: Messines Ridge

The Messines Ridge, situated a few thousand yards to the south of the town of Ypres, had been taken by the Germans in 1914 and they had fought tenaciously to keep it ever since. Strategically this ridge was hugely important; although at 260 feet above sea level it was no Mount Everest, it still offered whoever sat on top of it commanding views across the flat Flanders plains. If Haig was to push the Germans out of this area, he needed one of two things; either the British take control of the ridge by physically kicking the Germans off of it, or level the ridge completely, thus taking it out of the equation.

Such was the difficulty of any offensive succeeding in taking a large piece of heavily defended high ground, that the British High Command deemed it easier to alter the geography of Flanders than launch an offensive. So plans were put in place to blow Messines Ridge (and as many Germans as possible) to Kingdom Come.

The first tunnels had been started in the summer of 1915, and over the years and months these tunnels were drawn out and extended, culminating in over 8000m of deep tunnels, packed with twenty-one separate mines. By zero hour, in early June 1917, there would be 500 tons of explosives ready to rip apart the ridge. It was not all straightforward, however. The Germans were counter-mining too, and in some areas the enemy's work could be heard clearly. All in all, during the height of mining activity in 1916, there were about 20,000 British, Canadian, Australian and New Zealand tunnellers digging deadly holes in the Ridge, with about as many Germans tunnelling straight towards them. The tension of this underground war was not helped by terrible working conditions with tunnels frequently flooding, collapsing, or filling with gas, even without German meddling.

Slowly, each tunnel was completed and the explosives were laid. Many sat in situ for several months waiting for zero hour, which was destined to be 7th June 1917.

The plan was not dis-similar to other British attacks: A dirty great big artillery bombardment, followed by the blowing of the mines, followed by the infantry (some 80,000 British and ANZAC men in this instance) who would spring into action, with tank support, as soon as the mines went up. The main difference was that there was no breakthrough required, the infantry just had to take the ridge (or what would be left of it) and kill lots of the enemy while doing so.

On 21st May, more than 2,500 guns and heavy mortars let rip. Before long the Germans realised this bombardment was the opening act for something a bit bigger, and they rushed as many of their own guns as possible into the area and started giving it back to the Allies. The ensuing artillery fight was particularly savage, with millions of shells being thrown at each other day and night. British counter battery work was very successful and one by one the German gun batteries were knocked out. Then, just before dawn on 7th June the British guns fell silent.

Sensing an infantry attack, what was left of the German front line troops scrambled to their posts, manned their guns and waited.

At 3.10am the mines were detonated. The eruption was so colossal it destroyed an estimated 10,000 Germans instantly and was clearly heard in London and other parts of Southern England. Synchronised with the mines, every available gun the Allies had in the area started to fire a creeping barrage to aid the infantry attack. In retaliation the Germans shelled No Man's Land and the Allied front lines. The noise was impossible and confusion reigned, this was not going to be easy.

Following behind a steadily advancing creeping barrage the forward infantry moved towards the enemy lines. There were isolated strongholds that put up some resistance, but these were eventually eliminated, helped in no small part by continual harassment from the Royal Flying Corps and their thermite bombs which were being used for the first time. Thermite was a mixture of iron oxide and powdered aluminium, which when set alight set off a serious chemical reaction and threw lumps of molten metal everywhere. Soldiers suffered horrific burns as their clothes caught fire; trenches and dugouts made of wood also caught fire and caused massive damage. Chemical warfare had become even more brutal.

With the German front line captured, the Allies pushed on towards the village of Messines, which was captured after some intense close quarter fighting. By 5.00am all of the German defensive positions along The Messines Ridge had been captured. Soon after, the village of Wytschaete (or what was left of it as it had been almost totally destroyed by artillery fire) had been captured and the Allied forces were moving down the eastern slopes of the ridge. By late afternoon all objectives had been captured. It was now time for consolidation and preparation for the inevitable German counter-attack.

That counter-attack emerged the following day, but it failed and the Germans lost more ground as they were pushed back. Nonetheless the counter-attacks continued until 14th June, but without any success. By this time the entire Messines salient was in the hands of the Allies.

The victory at Messines was a much needed boost to British and indeed Allied morale. It was proof that a limited attack, if planned and carried out properly can succeed. It was far removed from the sweeping breakthroughs and epic victories promised from earlier campaigns such as on The Somme.

In just a few short months the defensive bastions of Vimy and Messines had been taken. The Germans were rocked; surely breaking out of the Ypres Salient was just a matter of time?

The Third Battle of Ypres: Pilckem Ridge

With the French Army in pieces after its mutiny, and Russia on the brink of revolution, the burden of the war was placed squarely on shoulders of the British and Commonwealth forces.

It was with this nervy backdrop that Field Marshal Haig was summoned to London to discuss the forthcoming offensive on the Western Front. It was a meeting that didn't go particularly well. The politicians didn't trust Haig and his team, and Haig didn't care much for politicians meddling into army matters.

Fundamentally, they were at loggerheads as to what to do next. The Prime Minister, Lloyd-George, wanted to move troops and guns out of the Western Front to the Italian Front in an effort to knock Austria-Hungary out of the war completely. With Russia disintegrating in the East, his intelligence reports suggested that Germany were re-directing troops and guns from the East to bolster the Western Front, a fact which made him uneasy. He didn't want another 'Somme' on his hands.

In the opposite corner, Haig and his intelligence team were convinced that in the West, Germany was on its knees. They were certain that the terrible battles of Verdun, Somme, Champagne, Vimy and Messines had taken its toll on the German army and that they were there for the taking. It just needed one more gargantuan effort on the part of the British, and the enemy would be swept aside, the war would be over and victory and glory would be his. Sorry, theirs.

The tipping point was when an excited First Sea Lord, Admiral Jellicoe, declared that because of the heavy shipping losses at the hands of German submarines, it would be impossible for Britain to continue the war into 1918. He insisted once more that the ports of the northern Belgium coastline be cleared of German submarines. The government couldn't argue with the Army and the Navy combined, and albeit reluctantly, gave their approval for the Flanders Campaign.

Ypres had become to the British what Verdun was to the French; a symbol of determination and a resolute defiance that would not be beaten. It would be at Ypres where Haig would deliver his knockout blow and put the enemy to the sword.

The tried and tested preliminary artillery bombardment opened up on the 21st July. More than 3,000 guns fired over four million shells over ten days in an effort to smash the German lines and barbed wire. At 3.50am on July 31st nine British Divisions (around 162,000 men) and six French Divisions (around 105,000 men) advanced towards the enemy lines along an eleven mile front. Their ultimate objective was the village of Passchendaele, some four and a half miles away. The main British advance centred around the Menin Road with their initial target being the ridge that dominated the flat plans to the east of Ypres. In the beginning, it seemed that the artillery barrage had done the trick, the troops advancing towards the ridge met with little resistance and quickly gained their initial objectives along the top of the ridge, and carried on towards St Julien in the north and Hooge towards the south. They met little resistance as many of the Germans had either been killed, or were running from their attackers.

However, the Germans had perfected the art of the strategic retreat. They knew that as the British advanced they would move beyond their artillery shield and straight into the mouths of their own guns. They pulled back, dusted themselves down and waited for the time to counter-attack.

At 2.00pm the Germans launched their own artillery barrage of epic proportions on to the advanced British troops, then their infantry launched a vociferous counter-attack that managed to push the advancing troops back onto the ridge.

It was at about this time that it started to rain.

The guns had never stopped firing in the salient since 1914, turning the whole area into a muddy moonscape of water filled bomb craters. The intricate drainage system in this part of the world was vital if flooding was to be avoided, but it had been smashed by the unrelenting guns and as a result the whole area was very prone to heavy flooding; the landscape quickly turning to liquid mud in a matter of hours.

When the rain came during the afternoon of 31st July it effectively stopped any chance of further advances. Attempts at a further attack the following day were also ruined by the rain which turned the Flanders lowlands into a mud churned swamp. No more major attacks were to be attempted until the middle of August.

When compared to the first day of the Battle of the Somme, the first day of Third Ypres, known as the Battle of Pilckem Ridge, was a definite success. Although the village of Passchendaele was not threatened, the British and French armies did succeed in gaining significant ground, and captured a strategic observation point in the Pilckem Ridge. However, once again, the cost was huge; the British suffered over 30,000 casualties, for an advance of just a mile or two. The French got off relatively lightly with 'only' a couple of thousand casualties.

It was becoming clear that the dashing advance promised by Haig was not possible; it would be yet another battle of attrition.

Bite and Hold: The Attack on the Gheluvelt Plateau

The rain that fell on 31st July continued unabated for seventy-two hours. The terrible weather put paid to any follow up offensive until the 20th August, although there was a limited but costly advance around Langemark between 16th and 18th August.

To be honest the Allied High Command were getting fed up with their attacks penetrating the initial German front line but failing dismally to get past the second and third line of defences. Perhaps it was time for a subtle change in tactics.

Enter General Hubert Plumer and his 'Bite and Hold' strategy which was devised to use the German plan of defensive counter attack against them. With the 'Bite and Hold' advance, there would be the obligatory monumental artillery bombardment, followed by the infantry advancing on foot, not in long lines as in previous attacks, but in small pockets of fighting groups, including specialist teams of bombers and rifle grenadiers that would take care of the German strongpoints. Another difference would be the limited scope of the advance. Troops would be ordered to advance 1,500 yards only, then to dig in. As a result, when the enemy launched their counterattack, instead of finding exhausted and disorganised remnants of the attacking force, they would instead run straight into a tight defensive unit.

Sounds like a plan.

Plumer was given the green light to put his plan into action and he had three weeks planning before zero hour on 20th September.

The target for this new style attack was the Gheluvelt Plateau, an important area of high ground that had already been twice captured and lost over recent weeks.

The preliminary bombardment opened up on the 15th with over 2,000 artillery pieces and field guns. It was the equivalent of one gun for every five yards of the front. It is estimated that these guns chucked over 3,500,000 shells, including gas, at enemy defensive placements, machine gun nests and artillery groups. The intensity of fire was three times that of the bombardment utilised on 31st July.

At 5.40am on 20th September the infantry, made up of British and Australian troops, went 'over the top' under cover of a creeping barrage. The attack went like clockwork, with the artillery bombardment working like a dream. Enemy opposition was quickly overcome, and apart from a small number of hostile machine gun posts that checked the advance in some areas, the first objectives were taken relatively quickly. After a quick break to regroup the infantry moved on to their second and third objectives. They then started to dig in and braced themselves for the inevitable counter-attack.

The counter-attack, if it had followed previous form, should have been launched around 8am. However the British bombardment had caused such chaos in the reserve lines that any new troops being brought in were not able to get near to the front line until late afternoon. This delay had allowed the British and Australian troops to move up their own reserves to help reinforce the entrenched positions. When the counter-attacks did eventually materialise, they were welcomed by a ferocious artillery bombardment and fresh troops. Not surprisingly these counter-attacks failed.

The Germans persisted for five days but the Allies held on. 'Bite and Hold' had worked, but as ever, there was a cost, 20,000 Allied casualties: killed, missing and wounded.

Polygon Wood & The Black Day of October 4th

The Bite and Hold formula was repeated on 26th September after more careful artillery preparation. This time the target was Polygon Wood, a heavily fortified wood, riddled with pill boxes and strong points which formed part of the German 'Wilhelm Line' of defensive systems.

Attacking over a shortened front line, which allowed for an even higher concentration of artillery fire, the attacking troops once again advanced relatively quickly towards their objectives. Each pill box had to be taken out individually, but the speed of advancement meant that often German troops were easily surrounded and surrendered without much of a fight.

By mid-morning almost all the objectives had been taken. German counter-attacks were once again decimated by Allied artillery fire. It was another victory for General Plumer and his 'Bite and Hold' strategy. Haig and all the senior staff officers were delighted with these results and urged Plumer to get on as soon as possible with the next campaign.

Conversely, the German High Command were worried. Their defensive tactics were not working, so Ludendorff altered his strategy and ordered front line trenches to be more heavily manned and fortified.

Plumer wanted to wait until 6th October for the next phase of his plan, however the weather reports were not favourable and he moved the attack forward to the 4th. Plumer also decided to dispense with the usual preliminary bombardment for this attack, asking his artillery to start firing at zero hour, when the troops would advance.

The initial advance didn't go quite as smoothly as the previous attacks. The rain had begun to fall, and some of the troops ran straight into a large bog, which meant they lost touch with their creeping barrage. Another section of the advance encountered heavy machine-gun fire at the edge of Houlthulst Forest, suffering over 1,500 casualties without much gain of ground.

The ANZAC's suffered terrible casualties in their own trench as they were preparing to go 'over the top'. With their front line trenches packed full of troops ready to go, the Germans opened up their own bombardment. After riding out this storm, the ANZAC's advanced into No Man's Land and came face to face with the German 212th Infantry Regiment, who were launching their own attack. Savage hand-to-hand fighting ensued in No Man's Land with the ANZAC's due to their superior numbers, eventually continuing on with their advance.

Despite these early setbacks, the tight co-ordination between artillery and infantry allowed the attacking forced to gain the German front line trenches before most of the defenders had time to react. Once more all Allied objectives were gained. The Germans lost 10,000 casualties on 4th October, mainly due to the new tactics initiated by Ludendorff which insisted that the German front line trenches were heavily manned. Such huge losses, along with 5,000 prisoners prompted the Germans to call this day 'the black day of October 4th.

Mandatory Suicide: First Battle of Passchendaele

There can be no denying it. The battles of Menin Road, Polygon Wood and Broodseinde were successful for the Allies. The German army was taking a hammering, becoming demoralised and there was even talk of tactical withdrawal. Haig sensed the panic in the German ranks and urged Plumer to renew the offensive, he was convinced the Passchendaele Ridge was there for the taking, and capturing that piece of land would enable his army to push the enemy out of Belgium once and for all.

Plumer set about planning for yet another advance, duly scheduled for the 9th October. As he did so the rain returned to Flanders with a vengeance. With its complicated drainage system completely smashed to bits, it didn't take long for the entire landscape to be transformed into a sea of endless oozing mud.

As well as reducing life in the front line trenches to abject misery for the infantry on both sides, the rain completely messed up Plumer's organisational plans for the new offensive. The rains meant it was almost impossible to re-arrange the artillery and get them in the correct positions to enable the proper support for the infantry. As a result many of the guns were stuck in their original positions, which meant they were having to fire at their extreme range just to hit the German front line positions. German artillery batteries were out of range, as were their machine guns. Not good.

The same issues of movement affected the attacking infantry. Movement was painful as the troops had to inch forward towards the front line over narrow duckboard paths. Every time a shell landed anywhere near these advancing troops the explosion would knock many of them off the duckboards and into the morass of mud, often sinking up to the waist and needing to be pulled out. It was a nightmare.

While the British and Allied forces struggled to prepare for their next advance, the German army were busy reinforcing their defensive lines. They had rushed reserves from the south to bolster the Flanders front. They may have been broken but with fresh men reinforcing the line, they were far from beaten. The rain continued to pour. Some senior British officers were in favour of cancelling the offensive. But Haig was desperate to seize the moment, and ordered that his forces would attack regardless of the weather.

His forces duly attacked at dawn on 9th October. The accompanying creeping barrage was woefully inadequate, and for the first time since August, failed to establish any kind of dominance over the battlefield. Ironically, as the advance began the weather cleared. The rain stopped and in perfect visibility the German machine-gunners cut the advancing infantry to pieces. With little or no artillery support the Allied advance didn't stand a chance. Anyone who somehow avoided being blown to bits by artillery or cut to ribbons by machine-gun fire found that the defensive belts of barbed wire placed in front of the German trenches were largely untouched. As a result, the offensive was an unmitigated disaster. Only in the very north of the line did the British and French enjoy slight success, but strategically it was of minimal significance.

However, not deterred by the artillery disaster, the continuing rain, the formidable defensive fortifications of the enemy, the thousands of dead and wounded still laying out in No Man's Land, the atrocious conditions and the slaughter, Haig and Plumer decided to have another go at the Ridge in three days' time. Yet again preparations were practically impossible. Senior Artillery officers approached GHQ and admitted they couldn't guarantee any artillery cover for the planned assault due to the extreme range and the instability of the ground making firing the guns practically impossible. Yet again the assaulting troops had a torrid time getting to their forward positions. Yet again Haig was asked to re-assess the planned offensive. Yet again he refused to waiver. The attack would commence as planned.

As zero hour approached the rain fell once more. Along a six mile front the assaulting troops advanced in a sea of mud. Once again there was little or no artillery support. In the eyes of the assaulting troops asking them to advance across No Man's Land in direct view of the enemy, with no artillery support, was complete madness. They were attacking elevated defensive positions riddled with pill boxes and other fortifications; they had no cover and had no place to hide. They were sitting ducks and the result was sadly inevitable; the attack failed miserably with the loss of 13,000 casualties in just a few hours.

And so ended the First Battle of Passchendaele. A distinct case of mandatory suicide.

Mud

The landscape rom the battered ramparts of Ypres all the way out to the village of Passchendaele was made up of almost continuous shell craters laying lip to lip. Horizon to horizon the ground was shattered by artillery fire. When the rains came, the result of such a constant battering was widespread flooding that transformed the entire area to a seething mass of liquid mud. Movement was rendered all but impossible – wooden tracks called duckboards had to be laid down to enable troops, guns and supplies to move to and from their positions. The trouble was that the Germans had control of the high ground, and in an area devoid of cover these boarded roads were in full view of their guns. These vital but fragile supply routes were continually smashed to pieces making life very difficult indeed.

Unless you were there it is hopeless to try and attempt to describe in detail what the battlefields around Passchendaele were like in the autumn of 1917. Unless you were there, to live and die in the fields of mud, it is practically impossible to comprehend what the soldiers went through.

With that said, the rest of this chapter consists of interviews with veterans who fought in the Passchendaele campaign of 1917. They have all been taken from Lyn Macdonald's masterpiece: 'They Called it Passchendaele'. If you have not read it you are missing an absolute treat.

Going up to the line for the first time my first indication of the horrors to come appeared as a small lump on the side of the duckboard. I glanced at it, as I went past, and I saw to my horror, that it was a human hand gripping the side of the track – no trace of the owner, just a glimpse of a muddy wrist and a piece of sleeve sticking out of the mud. After that there were bodies every few yards. Some lying face downwards in the mud; others showing by the expressions fixed on their faces the sort of effort they had made to get back onto the track. Sometimes you could actually see blood seeping up from underneath. I saw the dead wherever I looked – a dead signaller still clinging to a basket cage with two dead pigeons in it, and further on, lying just off the track, two stretcher-bearers with a dead man on the stretcher. There were the remains of a ration party that had been blown off the track. I remember seeing an arm, still holding onto a water container. When the dead men were just muddy mounds by the trackside it was not too bad – they were somehow impersonal. But what was unendurable were the bodies with upturned faces. Sometime the eyes were gone and the faces were like skulls with the lips drawn back, as if they were looking at you with terrible amusement. Mercifully, a lot of those dreadful eyes were closed.

Major George Wade, South Staffordshire Regiment & Machine Gun Corps.

The duckboards were slithery with mud and many sections were slanted to one side or the other. Sometimes there were new sections where it had been destroyed and the working parties had repaired it. Sometimes there were just gaps. We came to one gap, where a shell had landed. The bodies of three Germans had been laid side by side as a bridge In this hole. In order to avoid stepping into a sea of mud, we had to use these bloated bodies as stepping stones to get across.

Private C. Davey, No. 424129, 5th Canadian Btn., 2nd Brigade, 1st Canadian Division.

We heard screaming coming from another crater a bit a away. I went over to investigate with a couple of the lads. It was a big hole and there was a fellow of the 8th Suffolks in it up to his shoulders. So I said 'Get your rifles, one man in the middle to stretch them out, make a chain and let him get hold of it.' But it was no use. It was too far to stretch, we couldn't get any force on it, and the more we pulled and the more he struggled the further he seemed to go down. He went down gradually. He kept begging us to shoot him. But we couldn't shoot him. Who could shoot him? We stayed with him, watching him go down in the mud. And he died. He wasn't the only one. There must have been thousands up there who died in the mud.

Sergeant T. Berry DCM, No. 4406, 1st Btn., The Rifle Brigade.

It was in these conditions that the British High Command ordered their soldiers to attack The Passchendaele Ridge one more time...

Once More Unto the Breach: The Second Battle of Passchendaele

Deep down Haig knew that the Germans were far from a spent force. He privately gave up the idea of pushing the enemy out of Flanders and back to Germany; however he still thought there was validity in continuing the Passchendaele campaign. First, he wanted to seize The Passchendaele Ridge to get his army out of the mud and give them a better defensive position throughout the winter. He had also started thinking about a large scale tank offensive near Cambrai and hoped that by keeping the Germans occupied in Flanders he could achieve some level of surprise at Cambrai.

To carry out another attack at the ridge, and push onto the village of Passchendaele itself, Haig turned to his Canadian friends under the command of General Arthur Currie. Although he was not exactly enamoured with the task ahead, Currie did agree that the objectives could be taken as long as he was given enough time to prepare. Zero was pencilled in for 26th October and Currie got busy.

The grand plan was to capture Passchendaele in four short assaults of about 500 yards each, with several days in between each offensive to allow preparation time for the next push. The Canadians were as thorough as they could be in the time they were allowed. A new wooden road was built to improve logistics, new communication systems were put in place and huge efforts were put into ensuring the artillery was in the correct position.

As a result the artillery barrage that covered the Canadian advance was much more effective and by nightfall on 26th October they had achieved all their objectives. They were supported to the north by a mixture of French and British troops who didn't fare quite as well. The terrain here was awful; the men had to advance through some of the worst conditions of the war. Not surprisingly they suffered heavy casualties for little or no gain.

Four days later, the second push commenced. This time the Germans somehow knew about the attack and five minutes before the infantry were due to go 'over the top', they unleashed their own huge artillery barrage right over the Canadian front line, causing massive casualties. Despite this, the Canadians inched up the slope towards the village, their progress being severely hampered by stubborn defensive resistance, including particularly well entrenched pill boxes. By the afternoon, with Canadian dead piling up, quite literally, around these strong points, many enemy machine-guns were still active. Slowly, one by one, they were neutralised, and by the end of the day the surviving Canadians were just 500 yards away from Passchendaele village. Further progress however was repelled by swift enemy counter attacks. Meanwhile, to the north, the British continued to struggle to move forward in mud that was often knee deep. They tried all day to penetrate the enemy lines, but were simply cut down by enemy machine guns situated on higher, dryer ground.

It was left to the Canadians to take the village. On 6th November the 1st and 2nd Canadian Divisions eventually managed to reach their objectives and seized the majority of the village. The rest of the village and the remainder of the Passchendaele Ridge were finally in Allied hands by the 10th November.

Capturing the village of Passchendaele had cost the Allies in the region of 250,000 casualties. A quite staggering number. The end result was an awkward salient bulge in the line. The Canadian troops that held the salient could look forward to a winter where they could be fired upon by the enemy from three sides.

I bet they were well chuffed.

A Splendid Success... (Sort of): The Battle of Cambrai

Despite the calamity of Passchendaele, Haig was keen to sneak another battle into the end of 1917. The chaps at the Tank Corps had been itching to get back into the action and had been pressing Haig to launch a large tank-led offensive over some nice dry land since early 1917. Lieutenant – Colonel John Fuller from the Tank Corps (backed by the commander of the Third Army, Sir Julian Byng) had his eye on the area of land between the Canal du Nord and the St. Quentin Canal, however Haig had ignored his suggestion and had pressed on with his grand plans further to the north in Flanders.

With the failure of the Flanders offensive around Ypres, Haig was keen to end the year on a high, and turned to his new best friends at the Tank Corps and ordered them to deliver him a much needed victory before Christmas. Fuller and Byng got to work on the offensive, the plan was to launch as many tanks as possible directly into the jaws of the much fabled German defensive area known as the Hindenburg Line, with the important German held town of Cambrai at its heart – zero hour was pencilled in for dawn on the 20th November 1917.

At 6.20am that morning the guns erupted along a relatively short front. There was no prolonged artillery bombardment this time, Fuller and Byng wanted to surprise the Germans, but also a massive artillery bombardment would have ruined the relatively flat and unbroken ground and that would have severely hampered tank progress.

Almost immediately after the guns opened, the British massed infantry, spearheaded by over 300 tanks, rushed (at 4mph) forward towards the intimidating German defensive lines. It was the first time in the history of warfare that such a large amount of tanks had been used to spearhead an offensive operation, and their appearance in such numbers was initially very effective. The tanks were able to crush the barbed wire defences with minimal effort, allowing the infantry to penetrate with relative ease, by the end of the day an advance of three to four miles had been achieved on a six mile front.

The hitherto impregnable Hindenburg Line had been broken.

Such a contrast was this day to the hell of Passchendaele it was widely regarded as a spectacular achievement. The Daily Mirror summed up the mood of the nation, calling it a 'Splendid Success'.

However, it wasn't all that it seemed. Yes initial advances were impressive, at least by Western Front standards, however these advances were not across the entire front. To the south, the line had not been penetrated to any convincing level and towards the north of the line the cavalry failed to take advantage of the gaps that appeared. With 179 tanks lost in the first day, the impetus was quickly lost.

On the second day of the battle the Germans pushed a new division, fresh from the Russian front, in to the line where the British had had the most success the previous day, around the St Quentin Canal. Any more dreams of a cavalry breakthrough in this area were well and truly squashed.

Cue German counter-attacks. With fresh men, tightly co-ordinated artillery bombardments and pockets of well organised infantry attack groups armed to the teeth with mobile weapons such as light machine guns, grenades and light mortars, the momentum quickly shifted. Within a week the German army had recaptured the ground that was originally lost.

Technically then, this battle could be seen as a score draw, but with a total of 95,000 casualties across all sides, it was a costly one.

Kaiserschlacht I: Operation Michael

The situation Germany found herself in at the end of 1917 was somewhat mixed. Yes, the defeat of Russia in the East had released a huge number of troops and supplies that could be switched to the Western Front, but the window of opportunity for effective action in the West was rapidly diminishing as the Americans slowly but surely increased their presence in this area. It would only be a matter of time before they were ready to get in on the action in a meaningful way. The pressure was definitely on Germany to go on the offensive and try and win the war before the Allies got any stronger.

With this in mind, Ludendorff got working on his master offensive plan. His idea was simple: to smash the British Army to pieces.

The general consensus among the German High Command was that Britain was on its knees. The bloody offensives of 1917 at Arras, Messines, Passchendaele and Cambrai had, in their opinion, exhausted the British Army and made them ready for the taking. In their view, If Britain was out of the picture, the French would be forced to negotiate peace terms.

The rather grandiose code name for this offensive was Kaiserschlacht (*Kaiser's Battle*) which put even more pressure on them to succeed. It really was 'do or die'.

There were to be four separate German attacks on the Allied lines; codenamed *Michael, Georgette, Gneisenau* and *Blücher-Yorck*. *Michael* was to be the main attack, led by elite Stormtroopers who were to advance first in small pockets to exploit gaps and filter in behind the enemy front line, disrupting communications and supplies as well as sabotaging artillery. The massed infantry would then advance behind them and destroy the enemy front line that would be effectively cut off. The main thrust of the attack would run across the old Somme battlefields, towards the British lines and beyond, pushing them towards the coast. The other offensives were designed to be smaller affairs that would strike further north to take control of the remaining Allied ports on the French and Belgian coasts.

Operation Michael was pencilled in for 21st March 1918. 74 German Divisions (roughly 910,000 men) lined up against the British lines. The preliminary bombardment was a hurricane of just five hours where 6,600 guns fired 1,100,000 shells of all descriptions onto the British lines. The bombardment was incredibly accurate, both on the forward lines of the British, but also the reverse areas; smashing communication and transportation infrastructure as well as supplies and reserve camps. Not only did the British lose 7,500 in the barrage, but there was absolute chaos behind the lines.

When the guns fell silent a dense mist had enveloped the entire battlefield allowing the stormtroopers to penetrate deep into enemy territory undetected. The massed infantry followed quickly behind, also covered by the mist, and, despite some heroic defending by the British, over-ran almost all of the British front line areas.

By the end of the first day, the British had no choice but to execute a fighting retreat, they may have inflicted 40,000 odd casualties on the Germans, but they had suffered a similar number themselves and were quite literally, running for their lives.

The retreat continued through the night and over the next few days. The German advance was so spectacular and so ominous that The Kaiser decorated Hindenburg with the Iron Cross with Golden Rays, last awarded to Prince Blücher after the Battle of Waterloo. Surely it would just be a matter of time before they would be enjoying a victory cigar whilst strutting their stuff down the Champs d'Lyse?

The rapid advance began to falter however, after three days of chasing the British the German troops were exhausted and their supplies were struggling to keep up with the pace. German troops were hungry and were unable to resist the temptation of abandoned British supply dumps and helped themselves to chocolate and wine. For a moment the advance faltered, furthermore fresh British and Australian troops were being rushed into the breach. The defence began to solidify.

The Germans continued the offensive towards the vital railway town of Amiens but the defenders fought doggedly in a string of isolated battles.

The Germans had advanced forty miles, an amazing result in WW1 terms, but the land was of little strategic value, and they had lost a lot of men; around 250,000 all in all. And despite the vast tracts of land that were gained, the British line ultimately held out. Just.

Kaiserschlacht II: Operation Georgette (The Battle of Lys)

Even though the initial offensive had petered out a little bit on the Somme, the German High Command was itching for another fight. They desperately wanted to land the knockout blow on the British Army that would send them all packing off to Blighty, leaving the French with no choice but to surrender. They had their eyes on the Ypres area of the battlefield; in fact it was only the unpredictable weather and terrain at that end of the battlefield that stopped them launching the first big attack there. Before the Somme offensive had slowed down they were already planning for fight number two.

The plan was this – capture the high ground of Mont Kemmel and Cassel, drive the British out of the Ypres salient and push on towards the coast, cutting the British troops off completely. And do it quickly, before British and French reinforcements could be transferred from the Somme and other areas. Easy.

Because of the USA issue, time was of the essence and to be fair to the German Staff who were tasked with organising this offensive, they got their heads down and quickly produced a workable plan. By early April they were ready to go. The German attack zone ran from 6 miles east of Ypres in the north to 6 miles east of Bethune in the south – a front of about twenty-five miles with the River Lys dissecting the front 50/50. The guns opened up on the evening of 7th April and continued until dawn on the 9th, once the guns fell silent the German Sixth Army with substantial numbers of storm troopers leading the way, attacked.

The main brunt of this initial attack was south of the River Lys, in the area of Laventie and Neuve Chapelle which was, up until that day, a relatively quiet sector of the line, and held by the 2nd Portuguese Division. To be honest these guys didn't stand a chance, and although they fought heroically, they were quickly overrun, losing 7,000 men. The British troops situated on both sides of the Portuguese were tired and under-strength and it was no real surprise that they were also pushed back with heavy casualties, retreating almost three miles on the first day.

The Germans were rampant.

The next day, it was the turn of the German Fourth Army to launch their attack north of the River Lys. They quickly captured the town of Messines and pushed east. The situation for the British Army was desperate. On the 11th April Haig issued his famous "backs to the wall" order:

"...with our backs to the wall and believing in the justice of our cause each us must fight on to the end".

It made little difference; by the end of the 12th April the Germans captured Merville, now they were only 5miles from the important supply town of Hazebrouck and heading menacingly for the coast.

On the 13th April the Germans launched another attack in the south region, taking Bailleul in a bloody battle. General Plumer assessed the overall situation and, seeing that the southern flank was taking an absolute beating, he ordered his northern flank to withdraw from the Passchendaele Ridge, the scene of such enormous bloodletting just six months earlier, and take up new positions along the Yser.

Help was on its way though. On 14th April a change in the Allied Command structure saw the French General Ferdinand Foch promoted to General-in-Chief of the entire Allied Armies. This meant he had the authority to move French, British and any other Allied army around as he saw fit. He immediately moved French reinforcements into the Lys area to stop the advance on Hazebrouck.

Numerous small localised battles ensued over the next three or four days, but the tide was beginning to turn. German attempts to capture the high ground of Kemmelberg (17th-19th April) and to breakthrough towards the town of Bethune (18th April) were both repulsed by the British. Once more the German forward troops had outpaced their supplies; they were becoming weaker and running out of ammunition. This, mixed with the fresh Allied re-enforcements flooding into this sector, meant the offensive began to stall.

A second attempt to take Kemmelberg was successful on the 26th April, and further high ground was captured to the northwest on the 29th. However despite these isolated victories, it was clear the offensive was grinding to a halt and was not going to achieve its objectives.

On 29th April, the German High Command called off Operation Georgette. Each side had suffered about 120,000 casualties in twenty days of fighting.

Kaiserschlacht III: Operation Blücher-Yorck (The Third Battle of the Aisne)

Although *Operation Georgette* was floundering in Flanders, Ludendorff pressed on with his great offensive. Like a boxer switching his attack from head to body, he now set his sights further south, around the River Aisne and the Chemin des Dames Ridge. The Germans had lost the ridge in the Nivelle offensive of 1917, but Ludendorff thought that if he could recapture this area it would place his armies within striking distance of Paris once again. This in turn would force the British to move resources south from Flanders to help save Paris, thus allowing his German force to dodge back up north and continue their Flanders offensive against a much weaker defending force.

Basically then, this third phase of the great offensive would be nothing more than an extravagant diversion.

Holding this particular part of the line, were a number of British Divisions, resting and recuperating after being mauled in *Operation Michael* earlier in the year. Their commander, General Hamilton Gordon, had an inkling that something was about to kick off big-time but failed to convince the overall commander of the area, Franchet D'Esperay, to adopt the defence-in-depth tactics that had served the British so admirably in previous battles. D'Esperay was reluctant to give the enemy any ground at all without a fight, and demanded that the troops stay in their forward positions. As a result, when the preliminary bombardment of 4,000 guns exploded into life in the early hours of 27th May, the troops that were packed into the forward lines were easy targets. The German artillery decimated the ranks of the over populated trenches, in addition prolonged gas attacks against the Allied artillery positions nullified the risk of any counter bombardments that might threaten their advancing troops.

Mirroring the pattern of the previous offensives, the territorial gains on the first day were impressive. The defending troops were helpless against the massed infantry attacks and the line was easily broken. There was nothing for it but for an Allied retreat beyond the Aisne. So frantic was the retreat, and so closely pursued were they that they had no time to blow bridges or impede the enemy advance. By the evening the Germans had advanced a massive 10 miles.

Over the next week the Germans continued the advance, by 3rd June they had reached the River Marne and were only 55 miles from Paris. It looked like it was only a matter of time until they would steamroller into the French capital and knock France out of the war.

However, in a distinct case of deja-vu the German advance slowly outstripped their ability to supply the forward troops. The inability to supply the soldiers with rations and ammunition, along with general fatigue and a lack of reserves to replace losses, saw the German attack once more grind slowly to a halt just short of Amiens.

And so came to a shuddering end *Operation Blücher-Yorck*. Casualties were heavy, especially for the French who had suffered to the tune of 98,000 killed missing or wounded. In contrast the British got off relatively lightly with 'only' 29,000 losses. German casualties are not known, but are thought to be similar in numbers, around 130,000 killed, missing or wounded.

All along the line the Germans dug in, constructing heavy defensive positions that would allow them to sit tight for a while and await rations and re-enforcements. One such place was Belleau Wood, and in the ensuing Allied counter-attacks it would be the job of the French, with help from the United States Army to clear Belleau Wood of the enemy.

"Retreat? Hell, We Just Got Here": The Battle of Belleau Wood

The sheer ferocity and speed of the latest German offensive had scared the Allies witless. There was genuine concern for Paris and the future of the war. Reserves and fresh troops were quick-marched up to the line in an attempt to stem the flood. Included in these reinforcements were the US 2nd and 3rd Divisions, including the 4th Marine Brigade who took up positions alongside the French to the south of Belleau Wood, near Lucy-le-Bocage on 1st June. When the Americans arrived at the scene, the Germans were rampant and the French were getting on their bikes. The French commander urged them to fall back with the French troops, to which, Captain Lloyd W. Williams of the 2nd Battalion, 5th Marines uttered the now famous riposte: "Retreat? Hell, we just got here."

Over the next few days though, the Germans really put it on the Americans, culminating in a large infantry attack on 3rd June directly on the US positions, passing through fields and meadows in close order, with bayonets fixed. The Allied soldiers waited until the attackers were within 100 yards until they opened fire. The Germans had nowhere to hide, and as a consequence were ripped to pieces. The survivors were forced to retreat back to the relative safety of the woods.

On 6th June it was the Allies turn to put it on the Germans. The objective was simple; to kick the Germans out of the woods. The offensive would mean an infantry advance across the same fields and meadows that the Germans had crossed a few days earlier.

This area of land was swept from end to end with German machine guns, from among many positions, including a small rise of land called Hill 142. With little or no cover to be had, big losses were inevitable.

The first wave of attack jumped off at 3.45am, followed at 5am with the first wave of American troops making a dash for Hill 142, they had to rid this piece of land from the enemy to stand a chance of getting to the woods. Despite poor organisation (only half the troops advanced on time, the rest came up late just in the nick of time to rescue what had become a really bad situation) the hill was taken.

The second wave of Americans attacked some twelve hours later. This time it was a frontal assault on the woods themselves. In a grisly case of deja-vu the American Marines advanced across those same deadly fields and meadows where they had taken down the German infantry assault a few days earlier. This time, however, it was to be the German machine guns that were to have a field day.

The first waves of marines were slaughtered in the fields that day. There was no cover and no respite from the guns. Those that were not dead were simply pinned to the ground, scared to move. Then up rose two-time Congressional Medal of Honor winner Gunnery Sergeant Dan Daly, with rifle high in the air, he thundered, "Come on you sons of bitches! Do you want to live forever?" He then charged full-tilt towards the woods.

Not hugely eloquent, granted, but effective nonetheless. His fellow Marines followed and in a moment, an attack that was once floundering was now gathering a new momentum. By the end of the day the Marines had a small foothold in the woods. For his actions that day Daly won the Navy Cross and the French Croix de Guerre.

Marine casualties for the day were 1,087. Higher than any other day in Marine Corp history up until that point.

Over the next twenty days, the fighting in the woods was ferocious. Possession of the woods changed hands no less than six times until finally the Americans managed to kick the Germans out once and for all on 26th June.

During this battle the US Army suffered 9,777 casualties of which 1,811 were killed. It is not clear how many German casualties there were. In honour of the fighting that took place here, the name of the woods was later officially re-named to Bois de la Brigade de Marine.

Kaiserschlacht IV: Operation Gneisenau

The three gargantuan German offensives had definitely been tactical successes. Vast tracts of land had been gained, something not seen on the Western Front since 1914, and hundreds of thousands of prisoners, guns, supplies, rations and ammunition had been captured from the Allies. On the face of it everything seemed tip-top for Germany as the war moved into its fifth summer.

The thing is though these operations had almost brought Germany to its knees. Yes they had a windfall of extra men moved in from the Eastern Front, but with the huge losses of the first three offensives these reserves had been almost used up. The elite storm troopers that had previously broken through defensive lines almost at will had suffered terrible casualty rates, resulting in a sharp fall in good quality men in the massed ranks of the infantry. Also, the lack of any strategic cohesion to the offensive had resulted in numerous salients and bulges in the line, which not only stretched German supply chains to their limits but often meant the forward German lines were isolated and liable to counter attack from 3 sides. As a result these forward lines were left with a choice; fight off numerous counter-attacks or retire voluntarily in an attempt to straighten the line. To be fair, neither option was great for morale.

That said the Allies were not in the best of shape either. They too had suffered enormous casualties and the rate of German advance, especially towards Paris, was causing significant panic especially in French political circles where everyone started blaming everyone else and there was even talk of defeat and surrender. The British and French had always had an uneasy partnership, but the seriousness of the situation in 1918 had forced them to unify under a single supreme Allied Commander (the French General, Ferdinand Foch). Now the separate armies were able help each other out in times of need instead of fighting predominately solitary battles.

Allied nerves were shredded, tempers were short and tension was high. It was in this powder keg atmosphere that Ludendorff launched his next offensive – *Operation Gneisenau.*

The main objective of *Operation Gneisenau* was to flatten out the salient created by *Blücher-Yorck*. The attack would be centred on the River Oise and would be aimed squarely at the French Third Army. Unfortunately for the Germans, they were unable to keep the new offensive a secret. Confessions from prisoners and diligent work by French code breakers meant that they had a few days warning and were able to make some preparations. They reverted to the tried and tested 'defence in depth' technique rather than having the front line heavily manned. Also, they were able to lay down a massive artillery barrage of their own just before the Germans were about to start theirs. However, the German bombardment was enormous; 750,000 rounds of gas shells were thrown at the French, debilitating almost 4,000 French defenders.

At dawn on 8th June the German infantry attacked the French lines, advancing more than five miles and taking 8,000 prisoners. The advance continued the following day, and by 10th June they were just forty-five miles from Paris. The situation was becoming desperate once more.

Cue a surprise Franco/American counter-attack, launched with no pre-bombardment on the 11th June. Advancing behind a creeping barrage and with significant air support and over 150 tanks, they managed to halt the German juggernaut.

Ludendorff called the offensive off on the 12th after only four days of fighting.

The Momentum Shifts: The Second Battle of the Marne

Time was running out for Ludendorff. The four attacks he had launched so far in 1918 had most definitely pushed the Allies back, but despite repeated attacks to the south he had failed to draw the British Army from their northern base in Flanders. These offensives had cost Germany almost a million men, and the dual threats of economic collapse back home in Germany, along with the increasing US intervention meant that the only chance of ultimate victory was to launch another offensive.

Once again, he wanted to draw British troops south so he could attack with strength in the north against a relatively weak British Army. With that he planned another diversionary attack in the south, against an area held predominately by the French from the River Marne to Reims in the south, before hitting hard in Flanders against the British. This time though, he would have only a marginal numerical advantage (207 German Divisions against 203 Allied Divisions), there would also be no tactical surprise and the troops chosen to carry out this advance had already fought very recently.

On top of this, the Allies very much dominated the sky. There was little the German Air Force, which was short of men, planes and fuel, could do to stop Allied airmen flying all over the front, reporting back to HQ on German organisation and generally making a nuisance of themselves day after day.

As the reports came in, it became clear that there was something heavy going down. The French planned accordingly and requested British help, which duly came in the form of four British Divisions.

The German attack launched in the small hours of the 15th July. Twenty three German Divisions, backed up by 5,000 guns attacked east of Reims whilst another seventeen Divisions attacked to the west. The problem for the Germans here was that the French knew they were coming. The French forward troops had been completely withdrawn before the preliminary bombardment had a chance to wreak havoc. The idea was to lure the Germans into empty space within the French lines before launching their own counter attack. Indeed, they knew so much about the German attack, primarily from captured German soldiers, that they were able to put down their own artillery barrage on to the forward German positions which were packed with troops ready to go over the top.

The attack towards the east of Rheims was a disaster for the Germans and was halted before noon on the first day. In the west, however, they fared much better, making steady progress along a widening front and establishing a bridgehead over the River Marne. They managed to penetrate almost four miles before Allied reserves managed to stem the advance on 17th June.

The next day, 18th June, it was time for the French Army, backed up by the British, Italian and American forces, to give it right back to the Germans as they launched a rather juicy counter-attack.

Twenty-four Infantry Divisions, (over 400,000 men) backed up by over 2,000 artillery pieces, more than 500 tanks and over 1,000 aircraft hit the German lines at dawn on 18th June. They met little or no resistance and advanced over four miles on that first day.

Finally, after what seemed an eternity, the French were on the attack. A rejuvenated Allied force marched forward, slowly pushing the Germans back. Late on 20th June the Germans commenced an orderly withdrawal. By early August much of the ground lost during the German offensives earlier in the year had been regained.

Although the advances were not particularly spectacular they were significant; the initiative had definitely shifted away from Germany on the Western Front. Ludendorff's planned offensive in Flanders had to be put on hold indefinitely as he was now forced to be on the defensive for the foreseeable future

Casualties were once again high. France suffered over 95,000 casualties, Germany 168,000, Britain incurred almost 13,000 casualties and the USA was hit for 12,000.

A Black Day for Germany: Amiens, 8th August 1918

Whilst the fighting raged on the Marne, the Allied big brass were busy plotting what to do next. The general assumption on all sides was that the war would continue into 1919, but before the end of 1918 Foch wanted to launch a series of small-scale attacks to push out the annoying bulges in the line at St. Mihiel, Château-Thierry and Amiens. If these went well, then his plan was to seriously put the boot in with a grand offensive up and down the line.

From a British point of view, it was all going to happen at Amiens. Field Marshall Haig put General Rawlinson in charge of the Fourth Army which was based in and around Amiens and charged him with planning the attack on the salient.

The key to the success of the attack was to be secrecy and surprise. This would be the first time the British, Australian and Canadian forces would link arms and go over the top together as one, and it was a remarkable feat of logistics and planning that thousands of guns, planes, tanks and Canadian and Australian troops, along with all of their supplies and supporting functions, were arranged and placed in the salient under the nose of the Germans without them knowing what was about to hit them. With tens of thousands of men squashed into the front line trenches ready to give the Germans what-for, it was critical that everything was kept secret. If the Germans knew what was going on, a nicely timed artillery barrage into the Allied forward positions would cause utter carnage.

There would be no preliminary bombardment in this attack, no sir, instead new artillery strategies and techniques enabled the 2,000 odd guns that were pointing at the enemy to work a pattern that allowed them neutralise huge numbers of enemy gun positions, as well simultaneously laying down an effective creeping barrage that the advancing infantry could hide behind as they move forward.

At 04.20 on 8th August the advance began on schedule. The combined British, Canadian and Australian infantry advanced in good order, keeping close to the tanks that accompanied them on their journey towards the enemy. The battlefield was enshrouded in a dense mist; even so, slow moving tanks and massed infantry would have been sitting ducks for any kind of German artillery retaliation. However the German guns were eerily silent. The counter battery fire from the Royal Artillery were smashing the German guns to pieces, they had no chance to lay down any kind of fire onto No Man's Land. Very quickly out of the mist, masses of Germans came towards the attackers, hands in the air, surrendering. Many of them seemed quite pleased to be getting out of the fight.

In the centre of the attack, the Canadian and Australian infantry had advanced about seven miles by the early afternoon. Surely the tide was now turning.

It wasn't all plain sailing though, the German army may have been on its knees, but it was still capable of rustling up some formidable defence. Not all the German guns were neutralised. Pockets of resistance appeared up and down the line, consisting of machine guns and enemy artillery, not to forget the odd aircraft, and made the Allied advancement, particularly to the north (British) and south (French) very tough indeed. The British in the north had only a handful of tanks and were advancing over much rougher ground, which slowed the tanks down to a crawl. Although the first objectives were taken and an advance of two miles achieved, the attack soon petered out and they failed to take the high ground around Chipilly.

By the end of the day estimated German losses were 30,000 with the Allies losing 8,800. There were also almost 20,000 German prisoners taken, a statistic that lead Ludendorff to remark that this day, the first day of the Battle of Amiens, was 'the black day of the German Army'.

The fighting continued on the 9th but the extravagant successes of the previous day were not repeated. Supply and communication systems that were developed for static trench warfare were struggling to cope with the new found fluidity and mobility of the current operations. Roads were congested, they had outrun the artillery, tanks were breaking down and being taken out by enemy fire. Also, German reserves were beginning to flood into the area. The offensive was slowly grinding to a halt.

By the 11th of August the strength of the Tank Corp was a measly six, out of an originally starting number of over 500. Rawlinson recognised that anymore attempts at advancing would be useless and proposed that the focus of the attack be switched to the neighbouring Third Army.

The Battle of the Amiens was over.

Germany had lost 50,000 men in this battle, of which almost 30,000 were taken prisoner. On the 11th August Ludendorff met with the Kaiser and told him bluntly that the war was lost. He offered his resignation but it was declined. Germany was in all sorts of trouble.

In the meantime, the Allies were busy preparing another large offensive. It was time to turn the screw.

Back on the Somme: The Second Battle of Albert

In reality, the fighting never really stopped after the 'official' ending of the Battle of Amiens, although it wasn't until 21st August that the next big attack was launched. This time it was the turn of the British Third Army, led by General Sir Julian Byng to have a go, whilst being ably supported by Rawlinson and his Fourth Army.

The advance bore remarkable similarities to the Rawlinson attack of a few weeks back. Again there was no preliminary bombardment, the advance was once more led by tanks, and there was even another thick mist to shield the attackers from the vision of the defending machine-gunners.

The grounds they were now fighting over were the old battlefields of 1916 that witnessed such suffering and death just two years before. The ground was a tortured mess of old trenches, dug-outs, barbed wire and shell holes.

The first wave of the infantry advance went over the top in the early hours of 21st August, tightly grouped around their tanks as the creeping barrage brought down a lethal protective curtain in front of the advancing troops. The initial objectives were relatively limited, and once more the first wave was ordered to consolidate their gains and let the second wave pass through and press on the advance.

Progress was not as easy as it had been previously. The Germans were adopting a 'defence in depth' approach, often voluntarily giving up large tracts of land, often thousands of yards at a time, and using artillery and well hidden machine guns to break up attacks. The scarred landscape was a problem for the attackers, every shell hole, old trench or dug out was a possible hiding place for hostile machine guns, and so clearing the battlefield was slow and costly.

The terrain also meant that moving the guns further forward to support the advancing troops was easier said than done. The advance quickly out stripped the range of the guns and once they had done this they were vulnerable to attack themselves. Casualties were high as the Germans were well dug in and made the best defensive use of the landscape. Yet again the machine gun ruled the battlefield.

After nightfall the British consolidated their grounds and took a deep breath. In the meantime the people in charge of getting the guns, ammunition, supplies, rations and everything else nearer to the new front line frantically toiled in the background, making ready for the next 'big push.'

On the other side of the wire, the Germans, assessing the situation thought that the British had run out of steam and concluded (wrongly as it happens), that they were there for the taking. A counter attack was ordered for the 22nd. The German artillery flung over a vast array of gas and shrapnel shells, but the ensuing infantry advance lacked the intensity of the preliminary bombardment, and they were easily repulsed all along the line.

In the meantime, it was Rawlinson's turn, with his Fourth Army, to get in on the action. Their objective was to break up the German salient that ran from Albert to Bray-sur-Somme. Once more the barrage opened up in the early hours and the infantry advanced over the rough ground. Before zero hour Field Marshall Haig had given orders that each Division should act independently of each other to take full advantage of any weaknesses in the enemy lines. This was a marked move away from conventional offensive tactics. Encouraging groups of men to push on regardless of their flanks would undoubtedly result in more breakthroughs where the line was weak, but it also risked cutting soldiers off from the rest of the attacking force and exposing weak flanks for counter-attack.

That said, the attack was a success all along the line. German infantry were all too willing to surrender even in situations where they might be expected to fight on or at least execute a tactical withdrawal.

The attack was renewed on 23rd August along the whole front. Byng and Rawlinson joined forces and marched in the direction of Bapâume, taking 8,000 prisoners on route. The German army was in full retreat. Only the extreme heat was slowing down the advance, the tank crews were suffering terribly and many were near exhaustion, but the weather cooled over the following few days and they reached the outskirts of the town on 26th August.

By 29th August, Bapâume was in British hands and the Germans were fleeing for the safety of the Hindenburg Line.

The First Cracks: Central Powers in Trouble

By late September the Central Powers were in all sorts of trouble. On the Western Front the German Army had shot its bolt with their mammoth offensives, but they had largely failed to break the Allies and since early August the German Army had been on the retreat. An Allied offensive in Bulgaria had brought that particular belligerent to its knees and as a result they were negotiating peace terms. There were also talks of peace within the Austro-Hungary High Command, and the Turks were also toying with the idea of walking away from the fight.

On 29th September, the German Supreme Command had seen enough. They decided it was time to talk about an armistice. They were getting beaten up on the Western Front, and the naval blockade was making life very hard for the civilian population. Germany was not a happy place to be, the time had come to discuss an end to the war and an armistice with the Allies.

It was under this dramatic landscape that the German Army dug themselves into the Hindenburg Line, drew a collective nervous breath, crouched down in their trenches and pill-boxes, and waited; rifles and machine-guns to the ready for the inevitable Allied assault.

The German Army had been building the Hindenburg line since September 1916. It was meant as a general fall-back position if things on the Western Front became too hot. The general idea was to build a hugely formidable defensive line which the infantry could retreat to and rest up in relative safety, get some re-enforcements in, and galvanise themselves for another monumental scrap.

The original Hindenburg line stretched from Arras to the Aisne River, via St Quentin. It consisted of multiple trench lines 6,000 to 8,000 yards deep, hundreds of strong points and concrete machine gun emplacements which were all positioned in such a way as to provide a wide field of overlapping fire. And don't forget the barbed wire. Lots and lots of wire.

It wasn't a bad defensive line to be honest, and to plan a full frontal infantry attack to try and over-run it would be utter madness. Wouldn't it?

Well, the supreme Allied Commander, Marshal Foch, thought differently. He thought that if he threw enough men, enough guns, enough tanks, enough planes, enough shells and enough bombs at the Hindenburg Line, it might, just might, break. And if it did break, the Germans had nowhere to go; they had no other position to fall back to. A decisive victory would most definitely result in total defeat for Germany on the Western Front.

Foch's master strategy involved three separate offensives: A Franco – American attack between Verdun and Reims, a French, British and Belgian attack in Flanders, and another Franco - British tear-up between Cambrai and St Quentin. With numerous offensives happening within a short space of time, all the way up and down the line, the Germans would be given no time to rest, no time to move troops and reserves, no chance to think. Time was of the essence too, the attacks had to get going before the winter sets in, before the Germans had time to re-organise themselves and prepare reinforcements.

Thus the timetable was set: The French and Americans would be first into the breach on the 26th September, throwing themselves at the Germans towards the south of the line. The next day, the British and Canadians would launch an attack towards Cambrai, On the 28th it would be the turn of the French, Belgians and British to have a go once more at Ypres, and last but not least, on 29th September more British troops would be thrown against the St Quentin canal.

It was game on.

Breakthrough: Attacking The Hindenburg Line

Before the Americans could take part in the first attack on the Hindenburg Line, they had to shift an enormous number of troops, guns and supplies from St Mihiel, just a few miles south of Verdun, where, just ten days earlier they had taken part in a small offensive to reduce the salient in that part of the line. It was the largest American military undertaking since the Civil War, and although the Germans were already retreating from the salient when the attack commenced, it was deemed an important political success. Almost half a million men, 90,000 horses, 3,980 guns and 900,000 tons of supplies were transferred in up-most secrecy to their new positions, alongside another 220,000 French troops. Their grandiose objective was to charge through the multiple layers of the German defence line, and push north over thirty-five miles towards the vital railway junction at Mézières. Capturing this railway junction would offer up the prospect of cutting off the entre German Second Army.

The guns, (almost 5,000 of them) along with 500 odd aircraft kicked into life for the preliminary bombardment around midnight. At 5.30 in the morning, the combined American and French troops went over the top, closely supported by over 700 tanks, and advanced on the German positions. Despite the inexperience of the American troops and the fatigue and weariness of the French Army, initial progress was very encouraging. The attacking forces outnumbered the defenders in this section by almost eight to one and quickly over-run the first lines of defence systems, advancing almost four miles in many places with over 20,000 German prisoners taken.

As soon as the advancing troops progressed into more heavily defended territory, it became a different story. Progress was checked in the maze of German strongpoints and pill-boxes. The battlefield got very congested and confused, which just made matters worse. Both sides threw their reserves into the breach, but the German line held. The offensive had ground to a total halt by the 30th September, with a general advance of only ten miles. A disappointed General Pershing renewed the attack on 4th October but the pattern of fighting remained the same for the rest of the month. The Germans clung on to their positions, and even counter-attacked where possible.

At 5.20am on the 27th September, towards the north of the front and facing a much stronger part of the Hindenburg Line, assault troops of the Canadian 1st and 4th Divisions along with infantry of the British Third Army left their cramped front line positions and advanced menacingly behind a creeping barrage. Right in front of the advancing infantry was the Canal du Nord, which, with its surrounding marshlands and numerous enemy positions overlooking the canal from all angles, represented a formidable defensive obstacle. It would be the pleasure of the Canadians to take the canal, backed up by tanks and copious amounts of artillery. The fighting was savage, but the Canadians did manage to cross the canal and passed well beyond their first day objectives.

Across other areas of the front, the British were encountering fanatical German resistance. Progress was slow and casualties were heavy, however they managed to rally, utilising specially trained engineer units to destroy strongholds and maintain the advance. In two days the attacking forces managed to advance six miles along a twelve mile front, taking 10,000 prisoners along the way, and with the canal captured, the road to Cambrai was open.

As Ludendorff struggled to get reserves to the Meuse and to Cambrai, the Allies hit again, with an assault on the old battlefields around Ypres on 28th September. The plan was to drive across the Ypres salient, previously abandoned a few months earlier, and on towards the Passchendaele Ridge. Based on the slaughter of the British and Canadian Armies at Passchendaele in 1917 these objectives were hugely optimistic.

But this was not 1917. This was 1918, and the tide was most definitely turning. Despite the massed troops in the Allied front line having to endure a counter-bombardment from German artillery just before they went over the top, the British and Belgian forces quickly over-ran the under-strength German defenders and advanced almost ten miles in two days, capturing 2,000 prisoners en route.

In two days the Allies had advanced further than the entire Third Battle of Ypres, including the complete capture of the whole Passchendaele Ridge.

The Battle of St. Quentin Canal

The final and perhaps most important portion of the Allied battering ram on the Hindenburg Line fell to the British Fourth Army, led by General Rawlinson, backed up by the French First Army, and a sprinkling of Australian and American troops. This time the attack was aimed right into the heart of the Hindenburg Line, along the St Quentin canal. The defences in this particular part of the Line were significant indeed, in many places over 6,000 metres deep, and thought by many to be impossible to penetrate by infantry and tanks. The German defences at the site of the canal comprised not only of barbed wire entanglements and traps, but this particular stretch of canal was eleven metres wide, was situated in a deep cutting of about fifty to eighty metres high, at the bottom of which was approximately two metres of liquid mud.

No small obstacle to be honest.

The main attack was planned for 29th September. The general idea was for the American troops to have a go first, attacking in the tunnel sector towards the north of the line. In the south, it would be the role of The British Fourth Army to try and break through.

Two days prior to the big kick off part of the US 27th Division were tasked with eliminating a number of German strong points. These inexperienced troops not only failed to take out their targets, but many troops were pinned down close to the German positions and were forced to stay there until the main attack joined up with them. This meant that in this particular sector the obligatory preliminary artillery bombardment had to be cancelled otherwise it risked wiping these US soldiers off the face of the earth.

When the rest of the 27th Division went over the top at 5.30am on the 29th they walked straight into a raft of untouched German defences. Confounded by fog, the inevitable result was chaos and carnage. American troops got mixed up with the following Australians and the confused and intertwined units failed to advance into the main system of the Hindenburg Line. Meanwhile German artillery and machine-guns cut the attacking infantry to pieces. The losses amongst these men were severe.

Slightly to the south, more American troops, this time the US 30th Division, had far greater success. They had significantly more artillery support which made a massive difference. As they advanced they came across a much weaker defensive setup. By midday, Bellicourt had fell and the Australian troops had successfully leapfrogged their American friends and were advancing nicely towards the guts of the main Hindenburg Line. The Germans did manage to rally though, and launched a number of ferocious counter-attacks which managed to check any further ideas of Allied advancement.

Further to the south, the main advance of the day was in the hands of the British 46th Division. The supporting artillery barrage was immense and smashed away at the canal. When the infantry advanced, they did so behind a creeping barrage firing 126 shells per minute which provided an extremely effective safety curtain.

The huge barrage had battered the canal to such an extent that much of the banks of the canal were smashed to pieces and made it much easier for the advancing troops to cross the canal with a makeshift array of boats, ladders and lifebelts.

The Germans thought the canal was impossible to cross, and when the British troops came bursting out of the fog the German defenders basically panicked and immediately fell back to stronger defensive points beyond the canal. Here, the offensive paused for breath as a renewed artillery barrage smashed these new lines and fresh British reserves joined the party.

By late morning the British were on the attack again and by mid-afternoon, the main Hindenburg Line had been breached. It was, without doubt, a magnificent victory.

The combined Allied forces were attacking all over the place – up and down the front, the much vaunted Hindenburg Line and the Hindenburg Support Line had been broken. It was one of the most remarkable successes of the war. Only the Reserve Line, known as the Beauvrevoir Line stood between the Allies and total victory.

The Final Push: October 1918

The situation was just as bad for Germany away from the fighting. The civilian population had had enough and there were cracks appearing in the usual stoic German outlook. Anti-war demonstrations and marches popped up like mushrooms up and down the country and huge public pressure was being put on the politicians and army alike to find a quick end to the killing.

At the beginning of October a new German government was formed under the liberal Prince Max of Baden. His first act was to reach out to Woodrow Wilson, the President of the United States of America and ask him to arrange the "immediate conclusion of an armistice, on land, by sea and in the air."

Wilson kept this initial conversation with Germany away from the rest of the Allies, he threw his 'Fourteen Points' into the mix as the basis of terms for the surrender of the Central Powers. These fourteen points were first delivered to US Congress in January 1918 and were intended to be Wilson's vision of war aims and peace terms. The points included such demands as the independence of Poland, protection in Turkey for minorities, the restoration of the Balkan states, the evacuation of all Russian, Belgium and French territory, an end to secret alliances, free sea passage anywhere in the world, and the setting up of the League of Nations to protect political and territorial independence of nations.

Harsh to say the least. But Wilson wanted to see if the German leaders really wanted peace or if they were just playing games.

The armistice ball was now rolling and the political big-wigs of all nations began a month long debate regarding the terms of an armistice. Everyone wanted something for themselves, whether that was great tracts of land, independence for their own country or simply to shift the blame of defeat onto someone else. As the endless chat continued in boardrooms and conference centres across Europe, the soldiers continued to fight and continued to die on the front line.

The rain had returned once again to Flanders making it very difficult for British and Belgian troops to continue their advance. Further south, in the Argonne region, the Americans were also struggling with their own weather induced transport and logistical problems. It was becoming a nightmare, not quite of Passchendaele 1917 proportions, but even so, advancement was painfully slow.

Added to the adverse weather conditions, another factor slowing down the Allied advance was the quality of men. The dashing, exuberant soldier of 1914 and 1915 had all but disappeared from the front line trenches. Those that had not perished in some foreign field were tired, disillusioned and thoroughly fed up to say the least. They neither had the energy or the inclination to continue the fight. The rest of the soldiers were raw recruits, their energy for the fight was high, but unfortunately their training and experience didn't quite match their enthusiasm. Their Commanders knew this – they knew that they couldn't force and cajole their men forward in the way they did a few years back, they simply wouldn't have coped.

Despite this, the burden of the advance was placed on the shoulders of the British Army once more. As preparations were put in place for another go at the Germans, they themselves were summing up their last reserves of strength and courage as they braced themselves for the inevitable.

The British had been knocking on the door to Cambrai for a few weeks now. Eventually, on 9th October they captured it, although by then the town resembled little more than a burning shell. It was an important breakthrough however, as it got the momentum of the attack going again, once more the Allies were on the march.

To the south, the French and Americans re-launched their stuttering offensive in the Meuse-Argonne area, and yet again found the going tough. Instead of rampaging through lines of defence, it quickly bogged down into a fight of attrition. The Germans were not going to give up easily.

As the attacks on the north and south rolled on, the Allies steeled themselves for a tougher test in the centre, towards the solid defence network around and behind the River Selle. Ludendorff had brought in reserves to this area and when the British Fourth Army went over the top on 17th October they ran straight into a formidable defensive set up and took heavy casualties. By the end of the day they had managed to force the German defences. They had penetrated 4,500 yards and took 5,000 odd prisoners in the process. After a couple more days they had doubled the advance and widened out on a seven mile front, reaching the Sambre River and the Oise Canal.

As the Germans fled, the Allied leaders in the field allowed themselves to wonder if the end of the war was in sight.

Surrender and Mutiny: The Collapse of The Central Powers.

It didn't take a genius to work out that the end was nigh for the Central Powers. In all theatres of war they were on their knees. In Syria the northernmost Arab city of Aleppo was captured on the 26th October. During the same day, on the Italian front, three Hungarian Divisions that were fighting by the side of Austria asked to be sent back home to Hungary. Their wish was granted and 24 hours later they were gone. Also on that fateful day, the Turks instigated peace talks on board HMS Agamemnon, a battleship that had taken part in the naval bombing of the Dardanelles in 1915. The formal surrender of Turkey was served on 30th October.

The Austrian army was disintegrating too, many troops were refusing to fight, and after taking a final pounding from an Anglo – Italian attack where they were pushed back to the Piave, losing 7,000 prisoners on the way, they decided to call it a day. On 28th October Austria formally asked the Allies for an armistice, it was ratified and declared live on 4th November. Austria was finished with the war.

Now Germany stood alone.

On the Western Front the Allies had been on the attack for 100 days. During that time the pressure had never let up, the Germans didn't get one moments peace. In those 100 days Germany had lost 188,000 men as prisoners to Britain alone, and another 196,000 to the other Allied nations. No army in the world could cope with that kind of loss, especially after 4 years of war. The German army was disintegrating.

Meanwhile back on the Western Front, the final great Allied attack was about to get underway. It would be an assault on the Sambre Canal. The British Third and Fourth Armies under General Rawlinson went over the top for the last time in World War One at 5.30am on 4th November. Under the protection of a particularly angry artillery barrage they wasted no time in routing the German defenders, who, apart from the odd pocket of dogged resistance, didn't put up too much of a fight. It was during the crossing of the canal that poet Wilfred Owen was killed as he helped and encouraged men to cross the canal in rafts.

By the end of the day the Allies had advanced ten miles, taking 10,000 prisoners.

It wasn't just the army that was falling apart. The Navy was also in crisis. German Naval leaders wanted to put to sail for one last time in a suicidal mission to fight the British Grand Fleet. The thinking behind this was it was 'more honourable' to go down fighting at sea than to meekly surrender on land. Unfortunately, the sailors had a different opinion. They were not too keen on dying just so the reputation of a few senior officers would be posthumously enhanced. Five times the order went out to put to sea. Five times that order was ignored. The Navy had mutinied.

Unrest spread throughout the civilian population of Germany too with uprisings and demonstrations taking place in cities and towns such as Lubeck, Hamburg, Bremen, and Kiel. Troops that were sent to quell the uprisings actually turned and joined in... it was Russia 1917 all over again.

Something had to be done. Fast.

On a tour of the front lines the German High Command realised the military situation was a disaster and to avoid total annihilation an armistice needed to be ratified immediately. Prince Max knew that the Allies wouldn't deal with the Kaiser and eventually convinced him to abdicate and seek refuge in Holland. In August 1914 the Kaiser had said that his troops would be victorious and back home before the leaves fell in autumn. The leaves had now fallen for their fifth time and many of those soldiers from 1914 were never coming home.

It was time for peace.

On 10th November the Kaiser boarded his royal train and rode out of Germany, ending 504 years of Hohenzollern rule in Prussia and Germany.

Armistice: The Final Capitulation

On 7th November the German Army Chief of Staff, Paul von Hindenburg, exchanged a series of telegrams with the Supreme Allied Commander, Ferdinand Foch, to agree a time, date and place for formal peace negotiations.

It would be at Foch's headquarters at Rethondes in the Compiègne Forest

The German contingent of Matthias Erzberger, the German Secretary of State, Count von Oberndorff, Major-General von Winterfeldt and Captain Vanselow of the Imperial Navy were picked up at the French lines and taken on a ten hour journey to the Compiègne Forest, where a train, complete with sleeping, dining and office cars, stood ready for them. It was the evening of 9th November and it would be here where they would work, deliberate and negotiate the end of the war for the next three days.

At first the German contingent tried to negotiate terms that were less harsh. Erzberger in-particular, played the Bolshevik card and, in asking for an immediate cessation of hostilities, said that his nation was on the verge of being overtaken by Bolsheviks, stirred on from Russia. (A subject that would become a reoccurring theme in German politics and history for the next thirty years). He also requested that the Royal Navy to immediately lift its blockade. Foch's answer to both requests was very simple.

'Non.'

The Germans had no choice but to sign the documents and agree to the terms set down by the Allies, the main terms of which were:

Germany was to evacuate immediately all occupied territory and German troops were to withdraw behind a line of the frontiers of August 1914.

Germany was to hand back Alsace Lorraine to France.

The west bank of the Rhine River was to be evacuated and a neutral zone was to be established on the east bank.

Vast quantities of war material were to be surrendered to the Allies.

All Allied prisoners were to be repatriated, without immediate Allied reciprocity with regard to German prisoners.

All German submarines were to be surrendered; but the Allied blockade would continue.

Treaties which Germany had signed during the war, such as Brest-Litovsk, were declared null and void.

The Germans were to accept war guilt and pay 'reparations for damage done'. This was to include all valuables seized from the invaded territories.

At 5.10am in the morning of 11th November the German delegation signed the fourth and final armistice of the war. As soon as the ink was dry Foch sent a message out to all of his commanders.

"Hostilities will cease on the entire front, November 11th at 11.00am, French time."

Finally, after 1,926 days of war, the guns fell silent.

An Armistice for Twenty Years: The Treaty of Versailles

In January 1919, after the dust had settled, the Allied leaders descended on Paris. Their purpose was to decide the shape of post-war Europe and also decide what kind of punishment should be laid at the door of the various members of the Central Powers.

Although 75% of the world population were represented at the meetings, negotiations were dominated by the 'Big Four' powers of Britain, France, Italy and the USA. That is until the leader of the Italians went into a sulk after territorial claims to the Croatian city of Rijeka were dismissed out of hand. After this it was left to British Prime Minster Lloyd-George, French Premier Clemenceau and the US President Wilson to figure it all out. Despite this smaller group they still found it difficult to come to an agreement on what to do with the individual members of the Central Powers. What emerged from these Paris meetings were a number of separate treaties (all named after Paris suburbs); Versailles (for Germany), St Germain (Austria), Trianon (Hungary), Neuilly (Bulgaria) and Sévres (Turkey). All of these imposed territorial losses, military restrictions and financial liabilities onto the Central Powers. Not least the Treaty of Versailles which dealt with Germany.

In the case of Germany, it was expected (at least by Germany herself) that the treaty would be based strongly on the 'Fourteen Points' previously drafted by President Wilson. However, negotiations between the three main leaders were far from smooth. Wilson wanted his Fourteen Points to be the basis of any agreement; however the French wanted to put the boot in and really punish Germany. France had been ravaged by war, hundreds of thousands of homes, farms and factories had been destroyed, and France wanted Germany to pay. They also wanted to make sure that Germany could never wage war again and pushed hard for severe military clauses, including a de-militarised zone on the French border which would be patrolled by neutral troops. Lloyd-George was caught between a rock and a hard place, privately he agreed with Wilson, but the British public were baying for blood and, from a political point of view, he had to be seen to be dishing it out. If he was perceived to be overly lenient he would have no hope in the next election.

The final version of the Treaty, all 440 clauses, was delivered to German representatives on 7th May. They were far from impressed and replied with a long list of complaints. Most of these complaints were ignored.

Part one of the treaty (26 clauses) dealt with the establishment of the League of Nations. This organisation was set up to avoid future war and maintain European security. The other 414 clauses dealt with the punishment of Germany.

One of the most important and controversial of those remaining 414 clauses required Germany to accept responsibility for causing the war (along with Austria and Hungary). Under the terms of articles 231–248 (later known as the War Guilt clauses), Germany was forced to disarm, make substantial territorial concessions and pay a big lump of cash by way of reparations to certain Allied countries, equivalent to around £275 - £300 billion in today's money.

Military clauses limited the German Army to 100,000 men. Conscription, heavy artillery, tanks, aircraft, and poison gas were also a big no no. German naval forces were limited to 15,000 men, and thirty-six ships (under 10,000 tons in displacement). No submarines were allowed and the import/export of weapons was also banned. There were no time limits set to these clauses, an omission used as a justification later on for German rearmament.

Territorially, Germany was being asked to give up 13.5% of her 1914 territory. In the west, the much disputed Alsace-Lorraine region was returned to France and the border regions of Eupen and Malmédy were given to Belgium. The Rhineland and the Saar regions were to be placed under Allied occupation, gradually reduced over fifteen years. Other significant territorial changes included Northern Schleswig being returned to Denmark, the province of West Prussia would be given to Poland, thus granting Poland access to the Baltic Sea via the 'Polish Corridor'. This corridor also meant that East Prussia was cut off from mainland Germany. In another move to restrict German growth and recovery, the strategically important port of Danzig became a 'free city' under League administration.

Harsh. But was it fair? The USA didn't think so as the Treaty was rejected by Congress. It was also rejected by China, but ratified by all other Allied nations in January 1920. On-going enforcement of the rules of the Treaty ultimately came down to Britain and France, with Britain trying to soften some of the terms and France demanding strict adherence. The people of France didn't think the Treaty went far enough, and Clemenceau was quickly booted out of office.

In Germany, feelings were also running high. Their first democratically elected Chancellor, Philipp Scheidermann, refused to sign the treaty and resigned. However a new coalition government, taking advice from the military, signed the Treaty in Versailles on 28th June 1919.

In a moment of prophetic, singular accuracy, French Field Marshal Ferdinand Foch, who was of the opinion the restrictions on Germany didn't go far enough, declared "This is not Peace. It is an Armistice for twenty years."

References, Sources, and Further Reading

Ten years ago, a reference section in a book such as this would be laid out in a very familiar and uniform way; title of book, author, publisher and publication date. Nice and easy. However, these days it is more complicated (or more simple, depending on your point of view) than this. Indeed, if I were being smug, I could just put one word under this section:

Google

A search on Google, Bing, or similar search engines will reveal an enormous amount of information (good, bad and indifferent) on any topic you care to discover more about. Regarding the subject of The First World War there are numerous sites, both professional and private, that can offer the casual surfer masses of detail on many aspects of the conflict.

The BBC has a wonderful educational site at http://www.bbc.co.uk/history/worldwars/wwone/ as do many museums, especially the Imperial War Museum (www.iwm.org.uk), the National Army Museum (www.nam.ac.uk), the Tank Museum (www.tankmuseum.org) and the RAF Museum (www.rafmuseum.org.uk)

As well as these brilliant professional sites, there are also some fantastic privately maintained sites. One of the best is Chris Baker's The Long, Long Trail (www.1914-1918.net) but others such as www.worldwar1.com, www.firstworldwar.com, www.ww1battlefields.co.uk, www.historylearningsite.co.uk have all been invaluable in providing inspiration for this book.

In addition to these websites a core number of published material has provided me with a backbone of information throughout this project; *1914-1918: The History of the First World War* by David Stevenson (Penguin 2004), *World War One: A Short History* by Norman Stone (Penguin 2008), *First World War* by Martin Gilbert (Harper Collins 1994) and *The First World War* by John Keegan (Hutchinson London 1999). As for other sources and further reading opportunities the following publications are cited and recommended:

For the run up to war and the early battles of 1914, a reader could do worse than look up *Retreat and Rearguard 1914* by Jerry Murland (Pen & Sword Military 2011), *The Guns of August* by Barbara W. Tuchman (Presido Press 2004) and *Ypres: The First Battle 1914* by Ian F.W. Beckett (Pearson Longman 2006). Tuchman has also penned a very readable introduction to the American Army's involvement in the war with her *Zimmerman Telegram* (Ballentine Books 1979).

For anything on the Eastern Front, the go-to work is probably *The Eastern Front 1914-1917* by Norman Stone (London 1975), similarly to get an insight into the world of the British infantry soldier or 'Tommy' as they were called, T*ommy: The British Soldier on the Western Front* by Richard Holmes (Harper Perennial 2005) is an amazing piece of work which places the reader smack in the middle of the trenches by using letters, diaries and the memories of the chaps that were actually there.

On the subject of Gallipoli and the Dardanelles Campaign, *Defeat at Gallipoli* by Nigel Steel and Peter Hart (London 2002), *Gallipoli* by Peter Hart (Profile Books 2011) and *Battle Story: Gallipoli 1915* by Peter Doyle (The History Press 2011) are all very solid reads if anyone is looking for more detail and in-depth analysis on this particular part of the war. On the naval battle of Jutland, Nigel Steel and Peter Hart are on great form with *Jutland 1916: Death in the Grey Wastes* (Phoenix 2004). For a more wider look at the naval aspect of the Great War, *Castles of Steel* by Robert K. Massie (Vintage 2007) offers one of the most complete and comprehensive analysis available.

Back to the Western Front and for the subject of Verdun the classic publication is without doubt *The Price of Glory: Verdun 1916* by Alistair Horne (Penguin 1993), Horne's work is backed up ably by Malcom Brown's *Verdun 1916* (The History Press 2003). The subject of the Somme is covered extensively with readers positively spoilt for choice; three books that any reader should locate are *Somme* by Peter Hart (Weidenfeld & Nicolson 2005), Bloody Victory: The Sacrifice on the Somme by William Philpott (Little, Brown 2009), and the classic *The First Day on the Somme* by Martin Middlebrook (Military Book Society 1971).

The often overlooked battle of Fromelles is done proud by Paul Cobb and his careful account in *Fromelles 1916* (The History Press 2010) which includes details of the recent archaeological dig in that area.

As with the Battle of the Somme, the titanic fighting during the second half of 1917 from Messines to Passchendaele has also been the subject to intense analysis. *Passchendaele: The Sacrificial Ground* by Nigel Steel and Peter Hart (Phoenix, 2001) is right up there alongside the brutal account *In Flanders Fields* by Leon Wolf (Penguin Classic 2001). Another stand out account of this particular phase of the war is *They Called it Passchendaele* by Lyn Macdonald (Penguin 2003). Macdonald has produced a series of books, one for each year of the war, where she has put together an amazing collection of stories and anecdotes from the soldiers who were there. They are the most wonderful reads and come highly recommended.

On the Russian revolution, the stand-out western version is The Russian Revolution 1899-1919 by Richard Pipes (Collins Harvill, 1990), but if you are looking for a more human perspective then *A People's Tragedy: The Russian Revolution 1891-1924* by Orlando Figes is remarkable if a little verbose at times.

The final year of the war is covered in great detail too; once again Peter Hart is at the front of the queue with his *1918: A Very British Victory* (Weidenfeld & Nicholson 2008).

Happy reading!

8629209R00100

Printed in Great Britain
by Amazon.co.uk, Ltd.,
Marston Gate.